URBAN ILLUSIONS

New Approaches to Inner City Unemployment

Michael Bernick

New York
Westport, Connecticut
London

Library of Congress Cataloging-in-Publication Data

Bernick, Michael, 1953-
  Urban illusions.

  Bibliography: p.
  Includes index.
  1. Unemployed—United States. 2. Urban Poor—
Employment—United States. I. Title.
HD5708.85.U6B47   1987   331.13'7973   87-7208
ISBN 0-275-92804-7 (alk. paper)

Library of Congress Catalog Card Number: 87-7208
ISBN 0-275-92804-7

First published in 1987

Praeger Publishers, One Madison Avenue, New York, NY 10010
A division of Greenwood Press, Inc.

Printed in the United States of America

∞

The paper used in this book complies with the Permanent Paper Standard issued by the National Information Standards Organization
(Z39.48-1984).

10 9 8 7 6 5 4 3 2 1

To SOL and ELLEN BERNICK

"And God gave Solomon wisdom and understanding exceeding much, and largeness of heart, even as the sand that is on the sea shore."

I Kings 4.29

Acknowledgments

In 1980, J. Anthony Kline served for three months as the presiding judge of the San Francisco Juvenile Court. "The stories were always the same," Kline explained, "broken homes, petty crimes graduating to more adventurous crimes, second and third grade reading levels."

Though Kline soon moved up to become the presiding judge of the California Court of Appeal, First Appellate District, he also launched into a series of projects aimed at breaking the delinquency cycle through employment. He was appointed to the San Francisco Private Industry Council, spearheaded new employment programs at Log Cabin Ranch (the juvenile court facility) and started Conservation Corps programs throughout the state.

Kline further brought to the subject of employment a questioning of the liberal "Great Society" approaches, and search for better policies. As Renaissance was on a similar search, I often called for his advice. He always was available.

In general, the persons who came through on inner city issues were not the city's vocal left who fancied themselves the most concerned, but two other groups: the labor unions (as usual), especially Walter Johnson, the head of San Francisco's labor movement; and the city's conservative businesspersons, especially Richard Thieriot and Leo Hindery of the San Francisco Chronicle, proponents of inner city business development.

Thieriot and Hindery do not seek recognition for their efforts in spurring minority business development (in fact they actively discourage any attention to their efforts). But they represent the business commitment to widening participation in the market system that is key to anti-poverty efforts.

There were few weeks that I did not seek out Harold Yee for his advice on building inner city businesses, or call John Rothmann, Lefty Gordon, Bob Price, or "The Chief", Mr. Soto, at 16th and Mission, who for the past twenty years has seen it all in the job training world.

Henry McGee is a professor of law at the UCLA School of Law, but is dedicated to inner city fuller employment, and he travels often to San Francisco for Renaissance activities. Hank McGee has never received proper notice of his understanding of and contributions to urban housing and employment. I hope that someday he will.

Writing a book that merges the worlds of academic writing and trade non-fiction is a risky enterprise. If *Urban Illusions* succeeds in doing so to any extent, credit must go to Alison Bricken, my (very patient) editor at Praeger.

Most of all, nobody could ask for a better partner than my wife, Donna Levin. Donna brought a novelist's eye to this book. Further, she was consistently upbeat and encouraging against all disappointments, as it is written in Proverbs, "her candle goeth not out by night".

Table of Contents

URBAN ILLUSIONS

A door had shut, the low door in the wall I had sought in Oxford; open it now and I should find no enchanted garden...

I had left behind me—what? Youth? Adolescence? Romance? The conjuring stuff of these things. The Youth Magician's Compendium, that neat cabinet where the ebony wand had its place beside the delusive billiard balls, the penny that folded double and the feather flowers that could be drawn into a hollow candle.

"I have left behind illusion", I said to myself. "Henceforth I live in a world of three dimensions—with the aid of my five senses."

Evelyn Waugh, *Brideshead Revisited*

Chapter 1

We Set out to Reduce Inner City Unemployment

"There must be better approaches to reducing inner city unemployment," Bill declared.

It was the summer of 1981, and I was speaking with Bill Russell-Shapiro, the San Francisco businessman and urban planner. We were discussing the limitations of existing antipoverty programs, particularly those for employment and economic development. Bill and I had been closely involved with employment and unemployment on the local level for the previous two years.

In the fall of 1979 I was fresh out of the law school at the University of California at Berkeley, with little interest in practicing law and much interest in establishing ways to reduce inner city unemployment. I was introduced to Bill through Leandro Soto, the director of Arriba Juntos, a community group specializing in job training. Bill was a major sponsor of Arriba Juntos, to which I had come seeking a position as a job developer. No position was available, but another opportunity arose through Bill.

Bill had started a small volunteer group of his own, known as San Francisco Renaissance, to encourage business and labor in San Francisco to focus on unemployment, and he asked me to join him. I took a position in law in downtown San Francisco and, with Bill, started to meet on the side with unemployed San Franciscans. We tried to use our contacts to place them into jobs. By 1981 over 100 persons were coming to us: delinquent youth referred by probation officers, Job Corps graduates, and, most frequently, people who heard of us through word-of-mouth referrals.

Why was I so drawn to reducing unemployment? There was no single incident in my own background: no father or uncle who had been thrown out of work or suffered long bouts of unemployment. My father has been in academia, for over 30 years at the University of Southern California. He always has had a steady, secure job.

On the other hand, as far back as I can remember, work seemed to me central to well-being. I was bored and restless when I had nothing to do, everything then seemed stale and flat. As I looked out across society, it seemed such a waste to have persons idle.

I grew up in the Fairfax district of Los Angeles during the late 1950s and early 1960s. The Fairfax was a heavily Jewish district, some distance from the lower income areas of Los Angeles such as Watts and South Central Los Angeles. My first extensive contact with people from these areas came in 1965 at age 13, when I joined the Los Angeles Police Academy Marching Band as a trombone player. The police band was composed of 90 young men aged 13 to 19—one third or so drawn from largely white areas like Fairfax, Eagle Rock, Montebello; two-thirds from East Los Angeles, South Central Los Angeles and Watts.

The band administration was located at the juvenile hall downtown, and many of the young men were recruited from those involved in criminal activity and brought to the hall. Participation in the band and its highly disciplined environment was seen as a positive environment for youths.

The five of us from Fairfax car-pooled each Monday night to the corner of Crenshaw and Western in the largely black Crenshaw district, where we and others from the Crenshaw neighborhood were taken in police buses to a practice field near the University of Southern California campus. During the next three years I spent a lot of time in band activities: parades on most weekends, trips twice a year to state and national American Legion conventions.

I remember the band for two main features. One was the military marching style. For days I would walk around making the crisp military corners that we executed in the band. The other feature was the interracial camaraderie. The band was the first time in my 13 years, and one of the few times other than in sports teams in the years since, that I was part of an environment in which persons of different races worked together in equal position. The leadership positions, captain and lieutenant, were distributed among the various races, as were the lead musical positions. There were animosities among band members, but they were not split among racial lines, and there was a more general unity behind the goal of making the band the parade champion and American Legion champion. Though I didn't consciously think of employment or unemployment at the time, later, whenever I read about inner city unemployment, I would think of the band members I knew. The young men I knew in the police band showed persistence in pursuing a goal, regular attendance, hard work, and determination. Couldn't they be working in steady jobs?

During my undergraduate years at Harvard in the early 1970s, I spent the summers in Los Angeles as a meter reader for the Department of Water and Power. Especially during the first summer, the job involved walking through the lower-income South and Central Los Angeles, entering homes to read electric meters. At 10 or 11 in the morning I would see men and women hanging around, watching television, seemingly with nowhere to go, not infrequently arguing or yelling at children. Wouldn't the men, women, and children all be better off if the adults were working?

After college I spent two years very far from inner city unemployment, studying political theory at Balliol College, Oxford University. There I immersed myself in writings on the major political ideas- "community," "equality," "liberty," and through his essay "Two Concepts of Liberty" first met Sir Isaiah Berlin. In the gray world that much of political theory had become, Berlin's writing was a brilliant sun. He was a man of great knowledge, and he used this knowledge not in a pedantic fashion but to illuminate important political issues.

I read through Berlin's writings on history, philosophy, and government and in my final month at Oxford, got up the nerve to call him. I explained I was planning a book on the concept of fraternity, and he invited me to his house outside the university. His talk ranged widely on the use of *fraternity* during the French Revolution, by the utopian socialists, and in the present century. As I listened, I knew that I should strive toward an understanding like his: to push beyond the glibness that sufficed in politics, to understand issues with a depth and fullness.

The next years were spent following the conventional path of going to law school. In my final year of law school, I lived in Washington, D.C., completing a monograph on Judge J. Skelly Wright and clerking for one of the city's main law firms, Arnold and Porter.

During the latter part of the year, I was interviewed by corporate law firms and tried to persuade each that what I really wanted to do in life was to be involved with mergers and acquisitions, or management-labor law, or litigation. I was offered a position with Verner, Liipfert, Bernhard and McPherson, a law firm specializing in administrative law and political influence.

But as the time neared to start the job, the life of the Washington lawyer paled in importance to the unemployment I recalled in Los Angeles and saw daily anytime I left the northwest corridor in Washington, D.C. I had no idea of what I could do to change this unemployment; but I knew that (rather than law or political theory) it was what I should spend my time on.

At Arnold and Porter, my time was spent almost entirely in the firm's library, researching memos on points of federal civil procedure or checking cases for recent developments. The library had large glass windows on two sides and an air-conditioning system that did not allow the windows to be opened. I came to feel as if I were in a bell jar, slowly losing life in this rarified environment so removed from productive work. I've got to get out, I thought.

I went to see Bill Spring, a former Harvard instructor who was President Carter's adviser on job policy, at his office in the Old Executive Office Building. I thought that he might help me obtain a position in the White House or the Department of Labor. Instead, he emphasized, "If you want to learn about unemployment policy, get out of Washington. Go work on a local level."

I thought of his emphasis on local experience a few weeks later when two stories appeared in the *Washington Post*. One referred to Stuart Eizenstat, President Carter's main advisor on urban affairs. Among the young law associates at Arnold and Porter, Eizenstat was known, and his position was a coveted one. He had one of the best resumes in the United States, Harvard Law School, partner in a prestigious Atlanta law firm, now domestic advisor to the president. He was quoted periodically in the papers on education or employment or health care. What a phoney, I thought. He hasn't accomplished anything in any of these fields that would justify his holding forth.

The other *Post* story was very different. It focused on a school-teacher who had taught in one of the lower-income Washington neighborhoods for over 25 years. A number of her former students talked of how she had influenced their lives through her constant encouragement, her warmth, her teaching ability. This woman has worked quietly in one neighborhood, I thought, and in contrast to Stuart Eizenstat, she has made a contribution to education. I could do the same thing in the employment field.

I returned to Bill Spring. With his help I managed to land a temporary position as an attorney at the Comprehensive Employment and Training Act (CETA) program in Hayward, California, outside San Francisco. When this position ended in late 1979, I moved into the city and began my partnership with Renaissance and Bill Russell-Shapiro.

Bill Russell-Shapiro was 32 when I met him in 1979. He grew up in Westchester County, was high school president, and attended Yale, with an eye toward a career in politics. At Yale, he was elected college president, but he also developed an interest in the community organizing efforts of Sol Alinsky. "I read about Alinsky's work, and I agreed with his view of low-income communities organizing to handle problems that they faced rather than being dependent on others, such as business, to make all decisions. I visited Alinsky and nearly went to work for him when he offered me a job."

Motivated by Alinsky, Bill went on to a master's degree in urban planning at the Massachusetts Institute of Technology. He came to San Francisco and launched into a variety of community anti-poverty efforts. He joined the board of the Chinatown Resources Development Center and became its first caucasian board president. He joined environmentalists fighting the downtown Yerba Buena development and became board president of Coleman Youth Services. When a local labor leader, Walter Johnson, approached Bill to form a community group for employment, San Francisco Renaissance, Bill quickly agreed.

For the first three years, Renaissance operated as a volunteer organization, emphasizing one-to-one placements. By 1981, though, our thinking was more ambitious. "Renaissance will link community representatives, labor, and business to produce new approaches to inner city unemployment," Bill said in September of 1981. "We will not rely on the government. We will obtain financial support for some activities from the business community. For other activities, we will operate our own businesses."

Bill himself was tentatively entering private business, becoming a partner in a barbecue restaurant. No longer focused on a career in elective politics ("I just don't see politics as compatible with a good family life"), Bill had joined with Carl English, a black firefighter, to develop Firehouse Barbecue. He thought businesses might also be appropriate for anti-poverty groups.

So did Jay Jones.

"You've got to meet Jay Jones," Bill's friend Jeff Wachtel said when he heard about our plans for Renaissance. Jeff had known Jay at the Graduate School of Planning at U.C. Berkeley, where they had been students a few years before. Jay obtained a double graduate degree in planning and in law, and, since graduating in June 1981, he had been working with the Black Professional Women's Association in Oakland.

Jay was full of ideas about employment, especially ideas about creating new jobs. "New businesses, that's what's important. That's where the jobs are."

Jay grew up outside Washington, D.C. and attended Howard University in the early 1970s. He came to Howard to be an architect but, by his senior year, was majoring in urban planning and urban affairs. As he explained,

The place I lived in Washington was near Fourteenth Street, across the street from a community lot. Many days, I saw unemployed black men gathered at the lot, standing next to trash can fires with nothing to do. That was one thing that made me want to deal with larger issues. I kept thinking, what a waste of human resources.

Also, at the time the Fourteenth Street corridor was going through urban redevelopment, with the old buildings being torn down, materials carted away, and empty spaces and parking lots created. Why not renovate these buildings and put the men to work on them. I hadn't taken any policy courses at the time, of course, to see why it couldn't be done, so I still was excited by possibilities like it.

Jay went west to U.C. Berkeley to major in urban planning and decided to add a joint major in law. He soon gravitated to the classes on employment and participated in a Berkeley study on job generation led by Professor Michael Teitz. The study looked at which firms were generating jobs in California. It found that contrary to popular thought, the majority of new jobs were being generated not by large, established firms, but by new business start-ups. Over 55 percent of new jobs in California were being generated by small businesses—businesses of fewer less than 20 employees—and over 75 percent by new firms— firms less than four years old. The findings were consistent with a recent national study by Professor David Birch of the Massachusetts Institute of Technology, which was shaking planning departments across the country.

Jay's interest in business was rooted in his family background:

My mother and father had been small businesspeople. They had a cabinet making shop and a gas station, so I had grown up around small businesses. At Berkeley I decided that the key to reducing inner city unemployment lay in new businesses and new jobs generated.

I liked the Renaissance idea of working without government funds. It meant greater flexibility and more creativity in designing programs. Also, I liked the fact that Renaissance itself was just starting, that everyone connected with Renaissance seemed open to experimenting, not caught in bureaucracy. To me it was the chance to put into practice ideas about business development.

Soon after Jay joined us, so did Dan Martinez, a 35 year old attorney, who had spent 8 years in the job training world. In the late 1960s, Dan had headed Horizons Unlimited, a Mission district program linking low-income youth with government-funded jobs. Later he worked with the city as a job training planner and attended Hastings Law School. He heard of our thoughts on Renaissance and offered to join. "With the Reagan cutbacks", Dan said, "job training groups no longer can depend on continued government money. They need new approaches."

Jay and I decided to leave our jobs in 1982 to become the full-time Renaissance staff. Bill and Dan became the first board members.

We had no dearth of inner city young people coming to Renaissance for jobs.

By 1981 a parade of out-of-work San Franciscans was coming through the law offices of Sedgwick, Detert, Moran and Arnold, where I worked as an associate. All of them had heard of the Renaissance network and were looking for one thing, a steady job. I had come to know personnel officials at a number of the major firms the insurance companies, banks, and department stores. A call to these people usually enabled Renaissance applicants to get through the door and to receive consideration. Most personnel officials were willing to look at applicants sent by Renaissance, for we had establishment credentials. Additionally, we made sure that these applicants had resumes and knew the basics about being interviewed.

In some cases the job leads led to positions. But in the majority of cases, the personnel officials had more than 30 or 40 applicants for each entry level job opening. The entry level jobs downtown for which most of our Renaissance applicants qualified—jobs such as messenger, mail clerk, file clerk—had no dearth of applicants, including college educated.

The difficulty in finding employment was greatest with the young men. Many of these were very bright and energetic. But the San Francisco office economy had little need for them. The unionized craft and construction jobs paid $12, $14, $16 per hour and more. But these frequently had long waiting lists.

One of these young men, who had attracted some local attention, was Anthony Johnson. Anthony came to the attention of many San Franciscans on July 1, 1981 when he was shot while trying to enter a bus illegally. It was a Tuesday noon, and he was on his way to a movie with a girlfriend. Not wanting to pay the bus fare, he tried to enter through the back door. But as he did so, an elderly white man who was exiting put out a hand to stop him. Anthony shook him off, sending the man sprawling. The incident attracted the notice of passers-by, so Anthony turned to leave. As he did so, the man took out a gun and shot him. The shooting received front section coverage in both the *San Francisco Chronicle* and the *San Francisco Examiner* and mention in news broadcasts. Anthony was interviewed from his hospital bed. Then he and the story faded from public view.

Anthony came to Renaissance two months later. He was 19 at the time, a high school dropout who had spent time at a youth reformatory for street robberies. He was not sullen or menacing, as were some of the young people who came to Renaissance from the youth reformatory. He was neatly dressed, enthusiastic about getting ahead, and he volunteered information about how he wanted to get a job and make money and buy a home with a swimming pool. He clearly had a great deal of intelligence that wasn't being put to use.

There were other young people who came to Renaissance in 1981 who were not so intelligent or quick. About one-fourth of them had very serious obstacles to steady employment. They could not fill out a job application or read above a fourth grade level, dress or groom themselves appropriately for a job, or be counted on to meet appointment dates. A poignant example of this group was Patrick Martin.

Patrick was referred to Renaissance by a probation officer. He was 23, out of work, and he said he wanted to work. Over the previous six years he had seen at least five or six social workers, probation officers, and specialists with the Employment Service.

He was well liked by all of them. But none had been able to find him the main thing he sought, a steady job.

It was not difficult to understand why. Patrick had the look of a street person: disheveled, with a nylon shirt, inexpensive blue slacks, and white shoes two sizes too large (at the probation office, he was known for his dress as "the clown"). He was not menacing, but he was slow of mind and speech.

His job goal in life was not high. He wanted janitorial work ("scrubbing floors, sweeping, you know, I can do that"). But even janitor jobs in San Francisco are far from easy to obtain. Many are unionized and pay $8 an hour, so there are far more persons seeking the jobs than jobs available. Patrick applied for a few jobs but was never hired. He spent most of his time sleeping late, watching television, listening to records. Prodded by his mother and sisters (all on welfare) to "make something of himself," he occasionally ventured forth to the probation office or social service agencies for job leads. However, whatever leads were available usually went to the brighter and more reliable.

Could there be a place in the labor market for Patrick? Could the energy and skills of Anthony and the many other Anthonys and Patricks we were seeing be put to use productively in society? Further, could this productive work be achieved through the private sector, without relying on the government?

These were the challenges we set for ourselves. Specifically, we had four ideas in mind: (1) develop job training programs that would link inner city young people to the emerging high-tech jobs, and do so with private, not public, funding; (2) develop new businesses that would generate new jobs and income for self-sufficiency; (3) develop entrepreneurship centers to enable many other inner city entrepreneurs to launch businesses; and

(4) through innovative counseling and training, reach the "underclass" not reached by most training programs.

Jay and I knew other attorneys who tried legal strategies to obtain fuller employment. Nearly all seemed to be flailing about with no positive impact. Some of them had gone to work for "public interest" law firms. They were suing this or that state agency, seeking greater welfare benefits or unemployment insurance benefits or food stamps for the poor. This struck me as a non risky path, but not one that created new wealth or helped low income persons to become independent.

Other attorneys had gone to work for the public defender. They saw themselves as helping the poor by defending poor clients against state charges. But I didn't want to be like them. They too didn't promote greater wealth or independence. In fact, often they seemed to be playing out their own bitterness at society rather than assuming a productive role. Through Renaissance, I wanted our skills to be utilized in productive work.

Renaissance received a $5,000 seed grant from the van Loeben Sels foundation and in February 1982 started full-time. There were myself, Jay, and Silvia Ramirez, a recent graduate of the University of California, Santa Cruz, who grew up in the Mission district. We were headquartered in the Mission district, a low-income, heavily Latino neighborhood near downtown.

On a rainy Washington's Birthday in February 1982, I moved my books and notes from the Sedgwick law firm to the Renaissance offices, and my heart dropped. At Sedgwick, like most lawyers, I had been spoiled. There were clean, well-equipped offices, with large windows and carpeted floors. There were secretaries handling typing and answering phones.

Our Renaissance "offices" were on the third floor of a building on Sixteenth and Mission. These offices consisted of three desks and a file cabinet. An English as a second language class was held next to us, separated by a thin divider. We did our own typing and answered our own phones.

It was not an impressive beginning. But we were fueled by the belief that we could do great things, we could solve the jobs perplexity in ways unlike anyone else's. In the first weeks young men and women began to find their way to our offices, looking for jobs. Both Anthony and Patrick came by.

We were off.

Part I: The Limits of Training

Chapter 2

Renaissance Looks to the Private Sector

The official from Apple Computer was clear. The company was providing computers to public schools, with the goal of one computer in each school. But Apple did not fund inner city training programs, as Renaissance was suggesting. "Whatever gave you the idea that we would provide funding for this type of training?"

As I hung up the phone I wasn't sure how to proceed. Apple was the fourth company during the month of May 1982 to turn down Renaissance's request for funding. We had spent the previous three months developing a training course in microcomputer repair and seeking private funding, not government funding. The Reagan administration was calling on the private sector to assume funding responsibilities, and this seemed a good approach to us. Private companies in microcomputers, for example, could benefit from trained personnel. We would not be asking for charity or going to the government trough. We weren't asking for a great deal of money: $15,000 for a pilot class of 15 inner city students. But each of the companies—Commodore, Atari, Altos, Apple—came back with the same response. Whatever gave us the idea that they would fund training programs. They had more than enough applicants for nearly every job opening. To meet their personnel needs, they did not need additional trained applicants.

The microcomputer repair training was one part of our envisioned inner city high tech training complex. The complex would link inner city young people to the emerging technician jobs, particularly those of microcomputer technician, office machine technician, telecommunications technician, and microwave technician.

These jobs were increasing in number both with the new office construction downtown and with the growing nearby Silicon Valley. New offices meant additional microcomputers, additional typewriters, additional communications systems, which in turn meant a need for microcomputer, office machine, and telecommunications technicians. Other technicians, such as microwave technicians, were needed in increasing numbers in Silicon Valley, the collection of electronics companies 30-40 minutes south of the city. The valley's economy was volatile but promised growth with the increase in defense contracting.

Not only were the technician jobs increasing, but they also sparked the imagination of and were within the reach of inner city young persons. Many of the young men and women who had come to Renaissance during the previous two years sought jobs other than in offices. Thirty years ago, they might have found employment in manufacturing or on the docks. But these jobs had disappeared. At the same time, other non-desk jobs, the craft jobs—painting, carpentry, plumbing—had long waiting lists. Technician jobs were non-desk jobs in which one could take pride in the ability required.

High-tech jobs such as electrical engineer or computer programmer require years of advanced education. But the basic skills for technician jobs, hands-on repair of the machines and the basics of digital electronics, can be taught within a four to five month period. Though more than thirty community training organizations operated in San Francisco in 1982, they trained mainly in the clerical jobs. None was training in the technician jobs.

We started with business machine technician, as we had a contact in the field. I had been given the name of Earl White, the owner of Earl White Platen, a small manufacturer of typewriter platens in the South of Market area. His father, the founder of the company, operated an informal placement service for unemployed business machine technicians. Earl continued his father's concern with job placement, and on the side tried to place out-of-work technicians.

The business machine repair field in the San Francisco area consists of 60 or so shops, employing 3-15 technicians. There also arc 14 major manufacturers, including Olympia, IBM, Xerox, Taylor Made, and Burroughs, who maintain repair divisions employing 2-30 technicians.

Earl was enthusiastic about the idea of a training class. He said that jobs were multiplying, business was good, and employers needed trained personnel. He brought in another business machine repair dealer, Vern Lesher, whose Lesher Business Machines sold typewriters and did repairs. Bill and I met with Vern and Earl in December 1981, and they volunteered to help us design a course.

In January we arranged a meeting with an advisory council of other local dealers recommended by Earl and Vern. Seven machine dealers appeared and lent support to the class. They too saw the need for training, particularly with the rapid change in the field. For years the field had been dominated by electric machines. Now these were being replaced by electronic machines, electronic typewriters, electronic calculators, electronic copiers. The dealers were not willing to commit themselves to specific job openings, but they were optimistic that they would have openings in the future.

Working with these dealers, and with a former business machine repair instructor living in the East Bay, we developed a course curriculum by late February. We then turned to the manufacturers and main typewriter companies for equipment and funding.

We wrote to IBM, Xerox, Royal, Silver Reed, Toshiba, and Burroughs. We presented our curriculum for training and emphasis on job placement. We offered to publicize the course as, "IBM's Program for Inner City Youth." or "Xerox's Program for Inner City Youth", or "Royal's Program for Inner City Youth." We estimated the cost for a pilot program of 15 students at $15,000.

None of the companies responded so after a few weeks I followed up with phone calls. At Xerox the district manager's secretary said that all donations were made at company headquarters in the east. Silver Reed and Toshiba managers repeatedly failed to return calls. Only Royal and IBM left open possibilities for funding.

With Royal in fact we were able to meet with the company president. Vern Lesher was the main Royal distributor in the western states, and, when the Royal president visited San Francisco in late April, Vern arranged a meeting for us. The president questioned Jay and me closely on the pre-enrollment tests we administered. He explained that past government-funded training programs for the poor had failed in business machine repair because many students did not have the mechanical aptitude. They would be trained but still not be able to compete. One needed to have this aptitude, or all training was of no value.

Jay and I thought that his views on training were narrow. The tests we had studied that purported to measure mechanical ability were of questionable value: they included questions about the directions of gears or the formulas for acceleration. But we said nothing, for we hoped that Royal might be of help. Unfortunately, our obsequiousness proved to be of little value. A letter and two phone calls to Royal went unanswered.

The community relations manager from IBM did return our calls and referred our application to the equal opportunities program manager. A month passed with no notice, and I finally called the program manager. Oh yes, he had sent the application to the branch manager. Another month and a half passed again with no notice. This time the call to the branch manager brought the information that the application had been sent to the administration operations manager. Finally, five months after the initial application, the administration operations manager did contact us and set an appointment for 1:00 p.m. the following Tuesday.

At 12:45 p.m. that day, the administration operations manager called. She was running behind in completing an assignment. Could we reschedule for the following Tuesday? The following Monday, she called again. Could we reschedule once more, for she had encountered a scheduling conflict?

Each time I tried to be positive. Yes, Yes, we'll reschedule. No problem. But after putting down the phone, I'd struggle to regain my confidence and momentum. These calls made clear how little others felt about what we did. Renaissance enjoyed no leverage. IBM could come late to appointments or cancel appointments or ignore appointments, and there was no accountability.

During my lawyer days, I would make calls with the expectation that they would be returned. The calls usually were returned because the other party had an economic self-interest in the matter. Now, few of the companies I contacted, like IBM, possessed an economic interest in inner city job training.

After six months, IBM did contribute a total of $500 to Renaissance's training. Over the next years, IBM officials did serve on our advisory committees. But after the IBM administration operations manager I no longer held such a strong belief in a private sector approach to training. Not only was the time involved in seeking funds great, but also we were in a dependency position. Like all dependency positions it fostered arrogance on one side and humiliation on the other.

We did start and build the business machine repair course by turning finally to government funding. What a contrast. The government job training sources on both the local and state levels responded to proposals for training within set amounts of time. They returned phone calls.

They also provided substantial funding, not on a charitable but on a contract basis. We received payments as we placed persons into jobs. Our first cycle of business machine repair received a $12,000 contract from the San Francisco Private Industry Council. Subsequently we developed other contracts for $100,000 and $160,000 with the California Employment Development Department and the California Employment Training Panel.

Our disappointment in seeking private sector funding for business machine repair training was repeated as we developed the microcomputer repair training. In March 1982 we started a process of contacting retail firms, such as Computerland and Computer Connection, as well as manufacturers such as Atari and Commodore. Would they have job openings for computer technicians over the next year? What qualifications would they require? Would they hire graduates of a Renaissance program?

Nearly all of the companies foresaw opportunities in the field. It was a new field: microcomputers had been on the market only seriously since 1979. But projections were for a great explosion—personal computers would be like television, in every home by 1990, was the oft made observation. Both retailers and manufacturers were establishing repair departments.

We formed an advisory committee of employers and designed a training curriculum. We took this curriculum to the larger companies for private funding. We offered to bill a training course as, for example, "Apple's Program for Inner City Youth." Once again, though, the proposals for private support were met with silence. In fact, among these new computer companies there was little recognition of what was meant by inner city training. When we spoke with the old-line San Francisco industries—the insurance companies, the banks, the brokerage firms—there was understanding of the mission of community job training organizations, even if the companies might decide not to contribute. Not so with the computer companies.

Once again it was government funding that finally launched the training. After four months of seeking private sector funds, we applied for a contract with the state Lockyer Youth Fund. One month later we had a contract for $50,000 to train and place 20 inner city young people into jobs. Over the next few years we developed other contracts totaling over $200,000 with the

California Employment Training Panel, and the California Department of Education.

As well as seeking funds, we approached the private sector seeking job placements. We did not ask companies to hire anyone sight unseen. We did seek a commitment at least a few jobs for inner city trainees who proved competent in skills.

This commitment was made in a few cases. And in these cases, as the microwave technician training, there was employment success. But in the majority of cases, employers saw no need to go out of their way to hire inner city trainees when they had so many other job applicants.

One example was Digital Electronics, a nationwide computer manufacturer. Don Green, our training director, first contacted Digital in December 1982. He was referred to several personnel officers before reaching the personnel director. The personnel director was upbeat, and an appointment was set for January.

Don was excited about the contact. He thought that Digital might hire four or five Renaissance trainees. Together we appeared at the Digital offices in downtown San Francisco precisely ten minutes before the appointment.

Our spirits quickly fell. The personnel director was out of the office. He had forgotten about the appointment. We rescheduled cheerfully. No problem. What else could we do.

When we did finally meet with the personnel director he was enthusiastic about working with Renaissance. The company was expanding its repair division and needed technicians. He would check with headquarters and be back to us in a week. Three weeks passed, and he didn't call. Don managed to reach him after leaving four or five messages, and he assured Don, "I'm getting right on it."

Two months passed before Don called again, and a district supervisor appeared at Renaissance. This man also was very enthusiastic. He spoke of having 10-12 job openings, and he discussed a special training course that Renaissance might do for the company. For Renaissance this would be the ideal training situation, with jobs guaranteed from the start.

We never saw him again.

A similar series of events occurred with Tymshare, a provider of computer time, located outside of San Jose, with a work force of between 800 and 1000 employees. Lynda Hirose, Renaissance's microcomputer training manager, and I visited the Tymshare headquarters—a clean, carpeted, smoked glass modern structure in the Silicon Valley style—and met with the personnel director and the assistant personnel director.

What we were doing at Renaissance was great, they said. They were behind the training of inner city young people, and had a need for trained personnel. Tymshare employed both assembly technicians at the Cupertino plant and field service technicians in Fremont. They would check with the supervisors at each location to determine company needs and get back to us.

We didn't hear from them for a month. When Lynda called, the assistant personnel manager said that she would be talking with the service managers the following day. This happened twice. The third time that Lynda called, the assistant personnel manager explained that the service managers wanted technicians with two or more years of experience.

Probably the low point in job development was reached when Don and I visited Fortune Systems, a major computer manufacturer in the valley. Don had spent weeks arranging an appointment with one of the division chiefs. When we arrived, the chief was at the plant but had forgotten the appointment. He quickly ushered us into a small conference room adjacent to the entrance. He listened to us for ten minutes as we made our pitch: we talked of our motivated trainees, about their willingness to work hard, about their skills in hands-on repair. He said nothing and clearly could not understand what we were doing. "You're not looking for jobs yourselves?" he asked.

Over time, as in life in general, persistence yielded results. We continued to contact Digital, Tymshare, and Fortune and over the next two years placed trainees in jobs at each. Don continued to contact the business machine dealers who first met with us in early 1982, and by 1984 they were hiring Renaissance trainees. Five of the companies also donated copiers and typewriters to be used in class.

But the job placement process generally was one of swimming upstream. In market terms we were not selling a product—trained inner city young people—that was very much in demand by employers. This was true even as we tried a variety of marketing gimmicks—slick brochures, newspaper articles and other media attention, appeals to altruism. Our opportunities for placements increased markedly as the national economy improved. But even with the economy soaring along in 1984, with unemployment nationwide down to 7 percent, nearly every placement was a struggle, with Renaissance trainees competing against other applicants with at least two to four years of college.

On one level most employers sought to increase their minority hiring. However, the hiring criteria they utilized, especially the written tests in electronics, worked against the hiring of young inner city men and women. The Renaissance trainees possessed the motivation and basic skills required to do the technician jobs. However, many other non inner city applicants also possessed these skills. The written tests, and the approaches to hiring favored applicants who possessed years of more formal electronics background.

There was a handful of companies that did pledge jobs for Renaissance trainees. One of these was Varian, a manufacturer of microwave equipment with over 5,000 employees. Varian agreed to hire 5 Renaissance participants as technician-trainees. The participants worked at Varian in trainee positions during the day. In the evening they attended courses in microwave technology arranged by Renaissance at the Microwave Training Institute. At the end of seven months, they would be moved into full-time jobs if they proved competent.

Renaissance received over 60 applications from inner city San Franciscans wanting to participate in the program. We did initial screening, and Varian exercised final hiring decisions. The five participants chosen were all from inner city backgrounds, though they were in the upper band of the inner city spectrum. All had high school diplomas, and two had junior college training.

All five participants completed the training. Four continued at Varian, and the fifth went to work at the neighboring Eastern Laboratories. How happy the participants were at these results; and how happy we were at Renaissance. We might as well have placed five thousand persons instead of five for the high spirits that followed. Jay and Lynda and the five participants got together at a Chinese restaurant one night, and Don and I stopped by. I pretended to give a speech, but everyone hissed, and we all laughed.

We set out to replicate the training arrangement with Varian. The classroom training enabled them to develop a theoretical base in electronics to rise above the assembler jobs. The trainee positions enabled participants to earn income while in training. Most of all, the promise of a job at the end of training was the best motivator for both the participants and the company.

We contacted the other leading microwave firms in Silicon Valley, Hewlett-Packard, Lockheed, Watkins-Johnson, Teledyne. The training would cost them nothing, and they could observe the trainees before full-time hiring. But none of the companies was interested. By 1983 they had started to feel the competition from electronics firms in the Far East, and hiring had slowed. Further, they had been receiving more than enough applications for the technician positions from people with college educations. Soon orders at the Varian tube division slowed, and Varian withdrew its participation.

Outwardly, I always tried to be upbeat at Renaissance. No employers or funding sources wanted to hear about our difficulties. Publicly, I talked only of the success of the Varian program or IBM's role on our advisory board or equipment donated by Xerox.

However, for the first time in my life, I was plagued with anxiety nightmares. Since I had been a high school and college cross-country runner, most of these had to do with running. In one, I was with a college team and traveling for some hours to a track meet at the University of Washington, but when I arrived, I couldn't find my shoes to run. In another dream, the race was about to start, but I couldn't find my way to the starting line. In still another, I was leading the race and running without fatigue, but suddenly took a wrong turn and was off the course.

Still, between 1982 and 1984 all was not frustrated hopes. With some private sector help and government contracts we built an inner city training center. Hundreds of young people came to us seeking work, particularly in the electronics field. Here too, though, all was not as we first envisioned.

Chapter 3

The Agam Painting

The Valencia Gardens Housing Project is a collection of drab three-story structures scattered over a square block. Like most housing projects, it is characterized by young men and women standing outside at all hours, leisurely tinkering with old automobiles or talking endlessly. Periodically, the main city newspapers send reporters to write stories about the drug dealing at Valencia Gardens, or good government groups call for cleaning up Valencia Gardens. But the stories and calls are forgotten after a few days, and life in Valencia Gardens remains the same.

Across the street, hoping to be a contrast to this disorder, is the Renaissance Training Center. The center occupies the second floor of a four-story building that also houses a sheltered workshop for the mentally retarded and the largest black-owned janitorial firm in the city.

The center usually is filled with movement throughout the day. Job applicants come in and out. Some are older unemployed workers, 55 years and over, and they come to the center's Experience Plus, a direct placement service. Most of the applicants are the younger unemployed, 18-28 years. They come from

Valencia Gardens and other housing projects and low income areas throughout the city. For them, the center offers a variety of direct job placements, literacy programs, and skills training programs.

The skills training programs, in microcomputer, office machine, and telecommunications technology, are the heart of the center. The majority of job applicants seek "to get into computers", which they regard as the future. The technician classes are announced through flyers to community groups and announcements on the popular radio stations. The greatest number of applicants, though, come through word of mouth in low-income communities. From the start, the center never has had a lack of applicants. From the first year onward, it has received over 80 applicants for each class of 18 students. In 1985 the center was receiving 100 applicants for each class.

Though Renaissance has no racial quotas, the center participants chosen generally reflect the racial distribution of the low-income population in San Francisco: 35 percent black, 25% Hispanic, 25% Asian, and 15% white. All are low-income and unemployed, and most have been in and out of low-skilled positions such as nonunion warehouseman, stock clerk, security guard. They are seeking "a job with a future."

Heading the center, and in charge of preparing participants for a job with a future is Don Green who came to Renaissance in 1982 at the age of 30 to head the first microcomputer technician class. Over subsequent years he has developed the center from 40 to 160 students a year.

At 6 feet 5 inches and 230 pounds, Green still looks like the high school and college basketball player he was. Through basketball he obtained his first job as a recreation director. "I found that I liked working with youth, especially low income youth.

Even when I was practicing basketball, I'd counsel the kids who came to hang around; you know, encourage them to stay in school, make something of your life."

After college came a series of jobs in the juvenile justice system that proved frustrating and boring. Don was a supervisor at a group home for troubled youths and then a counselor with the probation department. As Don reasoned,

There was very little we were doing with the youth other than keeping them in line. Most of the youth had no structure in their lives; they hadn't grown up with any structure in their lives. I thought we could reach at least some of them through the structure of jobs.

In 1982 I heard that a new organization, Renaissance, was doing job training and also trying to be self-sufficient, not dependent on government money. I liked the idea of self-sufficiency. I had seen other job programs that were dependent on government funds, and the paperwork they spent their time on. When I came to visit Renaissance in spring 1982, I was disappointed. I thought it was a large scale operation. Instead I found only Mike, Jay, Silvia, and a few job applicants in the corner of a large warehouse.

Though Don may have been initially unimpressed with Renaissance, we were impressed by him. He was enthusiastic and positive that unemployed young inner city men and women could be turned into steady workers through a job training strategy. He wanted to build an organization, not (like so many persons in the antipoverty world) only talk about what was wrong.

The training structure for technicians includes four months of instruction, three and a half hours per day, in the basics of digital electronics and hands-on repair. The training also includes intensive job search instruction—how to locate job openings, how to write a resume, how to prepare for an interview. "I think that technical skills are only part of getting and keeping a job. A more important part is motivation and getting along with the employer. That's what I try to teach Renaissance participants."

The center places on average 65-70 percent of participants into training-related jobs. During 1984, 84 participants went through the office machine and microcomputer technician classes. Of these 58 were placed in training-related jobs; 9 went on to higher education; 17 either dropped out during training or were not placed in technician jobs.

For the majority placed in jobs, the training process does mean a step up from low-skilled, generally low-wage jobs. The training process may appear simple, but even in successful cases, there often are many turns. Don and the other training directors offer a variety of services, as, for example, in the recent cases of Monica Wayne and Bernard Burt.

Monica Wayne was 24 when she came to Renaissance in early 1984. She was on welfare, unemployed, had one child, and had no significant work history. In her application essay she wrote, "My plan for the future is to raise a health child and to give him all he deserves by means of being employed."

Despite her poor English skills and lack of work history, Don accepted her into class:

She was one of the last participants I accepted. She had no electronics background, and no clear child care plans, a problem with many single mothers. But she told me, "I know I need a trade," and she was very serious, and so I thought we should give her a chance.

The first section of the course was digital electronics, and Monica failed the first three exams. Her math was below that of other students, and she was not quick to pick up the sections on electronics theory. She talked of dropping out, saying that both her mother (with whom she lived) and her boyfriend thought she should focus on raising her child. Don told her repeatedly that she had talent and could make it, and he arranged extra tutoring. Also, he arranged a part-time job for her at Renaissance during nonclass hours.

With the hands-on section of the class, Monica's performance improved sharply. She showed a real aptitude for repairing machines, and her performance was at the top rather than the bottom of the class. She completed the four-month training and, with a new resume, expectantly set out to find a job.

To Monica, Don was upbeat and encouraging, arranging five interviews for her with business machine firms. Privately, he was not optimistic. "She's going to have difficulty. For one thing, employers are wary of hiring a single parent because, if the child is sick or the child care breaks down, the parent usually does not come to work. Second, though she can repair machines, she is going to be competing on written tests against others with years of electronics."

Yet, after her second interview, Monica called to announce that she had been hired by a major employer, Spectra Office Machines. "I nearly fell off my chair with surprise and happiness," said Don. "When I called the personnel officer, he told how impressed he was by Monica's seriousness."

Bernard Burt was 35, older than most students, when he enrolled in early 1984 in the office machine repair course. Previously, Burt's education and work history had been distinguished by an inability to complete anything: he had dropped out of City College, dropped out of San Francisco State, not pursued a career in police work after graduating from the Police Academy. When he came to Renaissance, he had been working as a security guard at $5.75 an hour but wanted a job with a future. "He talked my ear off, about how he wanted to succeed and not go in and out of low-level jobs, so I finally accepted him into the class", Don recalled. Burt came to class regularly and always on time. In class, he took copious notes. He was a model student, except that he frequently questioned the instructor, suggesting that the instructor didn't know the subject fully. The instructor was a woman, and she complained to Don that Burt had problems with women in authority. Looking over Burt's history of failed endeavors, Don thought that Burt had problems with authority figures, male or female.

Don tried to talk with Burt about accepting authority, but Burt was clear that it wasn't his fault, he knew he had no problems accepting authority. Don was pessimistic about Burt's chances for placement success, and he was not surprised when Burt was passed over in the first eight interviews set up for him. "Employers were uncomfortable with his work history of never completing anything, as well as his tendency to talk on and on instead of answering a question."

Burt never stopped going to job interviews arranged by Don, and through his persistence he succeeded in obtaining a job with Taylor Made System. How happy we all were at Renaissance when we got the news, for Burt often passed through the center and most of the staff knew him.

Three weeks after being hired, Burt was laid off. The employer told Don that Burt had good work habits in coming to work regularly, and had a sufficient mastery of electronics, but he couldn't take directions. He antagonized the company's training director by constantly disputing with him.

"I couldn't believe it," commented Don, "after all the time I spent with Burt emphasizing the need to be a team worker, and to accept authority." Still, when Burt returned to Renaissance,

Don helped him arrange an interview with another major employer, Savin Business Systems.

The day after the interview, Don drove to Savin to speak in person with officials, urging them to give Burt a chance. The company scheduled a second interview, and then a third. Finally, a month later, the company agreed to give Burt a one day tryout. When Don called to find out the results, company officials still were unsure. Finally, after a week, Burt was hired.

Whenever a job placement was achieved at Renaissance, there was much celebration and slapping of hands in "high fives." In opposite fashion, whenever a training dropout occurred, there was much muttering and shaking of heads. Thirty percent or so of participants either dropped out or were not placed in training-related jobs.

For example, in a recent office technician course, 4 of the 18 students dropped out before completing training. One student missed classes repeatedly during the first three weeks for court appearances and dropped out. A second student, a woman with a child, moved from Hunters Point in San Francisco to Oakland and lost ambition to make the commute. Still a third dropped out to take a job at Church's Chicken. This student, Michael Edwards, 28 (having left a job as a maintenance man in Nevada to move to San Francisco) wrote on his application:

My interests are to become good at electronics, to learn a tread, to better myself. My goals are to be skilled in electronics. In the past I found something about electronics—how much it pays, where the jobs can take you and thought about it for a long time. Now my future is here, and it's time to put thing together.

Despite the misspellings, the essay showed a real ambition. When class started, Michael attended regularly. In fact, he usually was the first student in class, arriving 20-30 minutes early.However, a month into the course, he took a job at night at Church's Chicken. He said he would continue to attend class during the day but failed to do so. Don periodically contacted him, but each time Michael said he would come in, he never did. It may be that he regarded the material as beyond his reach (though he was passing the exams), or that the prospect of an immediate job overwhelmed his desire to achieve in electronics.

Looking at cases in which training did not lead to placement, there is no clear, single explanation. In some cases, especially the unemployed between 17 and 21 years of age, there was desire to make money and not sit through training. In other cases, participants had drinking or drug problems that prevented their completion of training, or they had girlfriends or boyfriends who felt threatened by their success and tried to prevent it. In still other cases, participant gained skills but still was not able to compete successfully in the labor market.

Two cases illustrating these factors are the training stories of Nate Smith and Anthony Johnson. They are worth looking at in some detail.

In February 1983 I received a call from Sandy Sykes, a probation officer in San Francisco. At the time, we were recruiting for a new training cycle in office machine repair. Sandy said that she had a man on probation, Nate Smith, who would be "great" for the program. He was enthusiastic about work, he realized what a good opportunity this was, and he would attend class regularly.

Smith was 32, with a long-standing alcohol problem. He had served 18 months in jail for driving under the influence (and injuring persons). After his release in 1979 he had been arrested twice, once for robbery (while drunk) and once for carrying a gun (while drunk). Still, when he appeared at Renaissance in March, he was articulate and earnest. Yes, he had made many mistakes, but he wanted to start his life again. Commenting on another ex-offender who had enrolled in a training program and failed to complete it, Nate said, "He blew a beautiful opportunity. He's crazy."

During the first two months, Nate missed only two days of class. He always wore a tie and sat in the front of class. His test scores were among the bottom fifth of the class, but in the midterm evaluation the instructor commented, "Nate tries harder than the rest of the students put together."

Without warning or explanation, though, Nate missed a week of class, then two weeks. Sandy Sykes went to his downtown hotel to investigate why he had disappeared. She found him staying with a woman on welfare. Both had been drinking.

At Sandy's office, Nate claimed that he wanted to complete the class, but the woman, Wanda, kept dragging him down. She kept getting sick and coming up with reasons to prevent him from attending class. He was reluctant to leave her, though, as she was a drug addict and alcoholic and would go to pieces.

Sandy wasn't buying this. She emphasized that he had to break from Wanda, or he'd never get out of the welfare culture. He couldn't help Wanda until he got on his own two feet, with a job.

Three days later, Don, Sandy, and I met with Nate at Renaissance, and he declared that he was making the break with Wanda. He wanted to get off welfare, and he now was determined to succeed.

He appeared in class the next week and assumed the role of serious student. Then without warning he disappeared. Don tried to reach him, but he had moved from his hotel. He gave no explanation, and he did not appear in class again.

As he was on probation, he contacted Sandy after a few weeks. She later helped him get a job as a janitor at the airport, a job paying $8 an hour. This lasted two weeks. Again he disappeared without notice. After two weeks, he appeared in Sandy's office claiming that Wanda had failed to call in sick for him one day (after she had promised to do so), and he was then too embarrassed to come to work. By this time, though, Sandy was no longer believing.

In March 1984, Nate was arrested once more, for an altercation that occurred while he had been drinking. Sandy visited him in jail. "He looked terrible, he had gone back to drinking heavily."

Sandy has worked with ex-offenders for years. Of Nate, she believes that "there's a part of him that really wants to succeed, but there's another part of him that's really weak." She thinks that he had the ability to repair machines but didn't have the strength to break from Wanda or alcohol.

One time when we talked about Nate, Sandy explained his weakness in terms of fear of success. She noted that he stopped attending only as he neared the course completion, that at this time he complained that employers would never hire him because of his record, even though Sandy and others emphatically told him otherwise. However, another time, Sandy downplayed any psychological interpretation, saying that Nate simply "couldn't get it together."

This was typical of the uncertainty that Sandy, Don, and I felt in most cases of participants not placed in jobs. Motivation, or lack of it, was nearly always at the root. But we were not easily able to pinpoint the motivation gap or what to do about it.

Similarly, with Anthony Johnson, none of us were able to link his considerable talents, and even drive, to a steady job. This energetic, bright young man who first came to Renaissance in 1981 and who was with us when we launched full-time efforts in 1982, wasn't able to complete training or stay with a job over the next three years.

In 1982, when we launched the first office machine technician course, Anthony seemed a sure success. Shortly after we opened our Renaissance offices in early 1982, Anthony appeared, anxious for work. We arranged an interview for him with Vern Lesher and Earl White, the chairs of our business machine repair advisory council. Anthony appeared on time and in a camel coat and tie. Earl and Vern were impressed by how clean cut and well spoken he was, and they arranged a job with a business machine repair shop downtown.

Anthony approached the job with enthusiasm. There were only three other technicians in the shop, along with the manager. Anthony made deliveries of typewriters. He also was taught the rudiments of repairing typewriters and given responsibility for repairing IBMs and Royals.

Not more than six weeks later, we received a call from the shop manager, upset about Anthony's work performance. Anthony had come late to work on a number of occasions, he had come to work with liquor on his breath, he had asked to borrow the company car at night, and he had offered to sell drugs to the secretary.

When Anthony came to Renaissance, he denied the charges. He maintained that he arrived late to work because he missed the bus. Also, he asked to borrow the company car because he needed to move one night, and he had only joked with the secretary about drugs. Anthony said he didn't want to lose the job, and when he finished talking he was near tears.

To Anthony, Don was firm. "There's no excuse for being late to work; and if an employer tells you to do something, you do it." But privately, he advised, "I think he should be given another chance." Don called the shop manager, who agreed not to fire Anthony.

Anthony went back to the shop, but he no longer felt welcome. He missed two days, without calling. When he appeared on the third day, the manager said he was fired.

We didn't see Anthony for two months. He had no phone in his apartment, so Don could not contact him. Then, a few days before the office technician class was to start in May 1982, Anthony appeared at Renaissance. He wanted to enroll in the class.

On the first day of class, Anthony was the star. He held forth on his experience in the field. "It's a great field. I fixed all machines, Royals, Toshibas. You can make $25,000, $30,000 a year as a repairman." I asked Anthony what he would do with his money. "I'll buy myself a house and a swimming pool," and the others in the class smiled in agreement.

Anthony attended class for two weeks. Then his interest waned. His girlfriend was pregnant, and he wanted to rent his own apartment on Potrero Hill. He wanted to make money. "I can't afford to stay in class."

Don helped him obtain a part-time job with Control Data Institute, a computer school, serving as an office aide. For three weeks, he appeared on time at the job and did not miss a day. But the job was only ten hours a week and paid less than $40 a week. Anthony wanted to work more and make more money. He decided to drop out of class and seek full-time employment.

We tried to persuade him not to drop out. He didn't need money immediately; he could continue to live with his father or grandmother. With unemployment running over 9%, he would encounter difficulty finding any job.

But he was gone. We didn't see him for five months. He then surfaced, recently released from jail on a drug selling charge. He asked for a job.

By now he was known among Renaissance staff. There was sharp disagreement whether to hire him in one of our businesses, the Renaissance Cable Division. Part of the staff thought that he had been given opportunities in training and at Control Data and not taken advantage of them. To hire him would suggest that he could lose a job and always be given another chance. Other staff thought that Renaissance should try to bring him along, to help him develop work discipline and a work history. This was a frequent dilemma at Renaissance: what new opportunities to give participants who had quit or been fired from previous opportunities. On the one hand, Renaissance shouldn't work only with persons who were well motivated and directed; on the other hand, Renaissance shouldn't become a crutch, allowing persons to avoid responsibility.

In Anthony's case, the decision was made to hire him. For the first month he attended regularly and performed competently. Then he disappeared for two days, without calling. His explanation: his girlfriend walked out on him, taking their son.

He was placed on probation and worked steadily for the next six weeks. At the end of ten weeks, he commented, "This is the longest I've held a job." Soon thereafter, though, his attendance became irregular. Efforts to contact him proved unsuccessful. This time he was fired.

Anthony reappeared at Renaissance three months later. He was now working in inventory at a women's wear warehouse near Potrero Hill. He had been working for three weeks, at $4.00 an hour.

He said that the job was okay but went on to ask about work in the Renaissance businesses. We recently had started a new one, the Renaissance Business Machine Repair Service, and when Anthony heard about this, his face brightened. Anthony said he still was good at repairing IBMs, Royals, Toshibas. Anthony said he wanted a full-time office machine job, so that he could make $30,000 a year. What about his previous jobs? The job at Control Data was only part-time, and the job at Renaissance Cable paid only $4.00 an hour, not enough to support his growing family. He wanted a full-time job.

There were no job openings in Renaissance Business Machines Service. Don did offer the opportunity to return to the office technician class, telling to Anthony that realistically he needed to expand his skills. But training wasn't for Anthony. He wanted a full-time, skilled job.

Later I learned that Anthony left the inventory job a month later. His in-and-out pattern in low-wage, low-skill jobs continued.

"He clearly has the intelligence, and personality to succeed," Don commented one day about Anthony. "He even has the ability that many ghetto youth lack to move between two worlds, to talk street and to relate in business environments. He just doesn't have a stick-to-it-ness for training. He might succeed in an on-the-job training situation. But what employer will take him with many other trained applicants looking for jobs. I'm not sure what we can do."

The Israeli artist Agam has a number of paintings composed of curved surfaces with various patterns and gradations of color. Standing at one side or the other of one of these paintings, you see only black and white. Walking toward the center of the painting, though, you see colors emerging. Directly in front of the painting, a full pattern of colors is present.

In similar fashion, from a distance or from side angles, the job training process can appear to be effective (Monica Wayne) or very ineffective (Nate Smith). The truth is more complex, with a few dramatic job improvements, a few clear failures, and the majority of participants placed in jobs, that are a step above the low-skilled jobs from which they usually come. The overall effect of this training is not a sharp reduction in the "underclass" or poverty. Those with serious motivational or personal problems only rarely are "turned around" in the training process. But at a relatively low cost ($2,000 per participant), the training does help maintain the channels of mobility and give some reign to talent and ambition.

In early 1985, Don spoke to a public policy class at U.C. Berkeley and was asked if he still believed in training as an antipoverty approach. "No question, I do. It's not a charade; the majority do get jobs." Then he thought for a moment and added, "Of course, there are the Nate Smiths and Anthony Johnsons; and I do pull out my hair."

Chapter 4

Reading And Writing below the Ninth Grade Level

All applicants to Renaissance business machine repair and microcomputer repair courses complete an application form. The last question asks, "What are your goals for the future? (Answer fully, please write at least a paragraph)." In a recent recruitment cycle, these were three of the answers:

"My is to get a good paying job, with growth potential in an expanding field; And hopefully I can later become more involved with electrical computers."

"To be a electronic clerk, and to go to college or maybe go to the service. If I don't go to the serive I'll probably go into the resturaunt business."

"For a man ho jush got out jail, with no future, I need some training and operationally."

The misspellings and grammatical mistakes in these answers are not unusual. In fact, it is rare to find a paragraph answer that is coherent and not filled with spelling or grammar errors. In one-fifth or so of the cases, applicants are not able to read the application forms. They devise explanations ("I've got an appointment." "Someone's waiting for me") to take the application home and have someone else fill it out for them.

During the past two decades, inner city schools have been improved in terms of equipment and facilities, but no similar improvement in achievement has followed. The majority of inner city children attending these schools are not mastering the reading and writing skills needed even to participate in skills training or the emerging entry-level jobs. To take advantage of Renaissance business machine repair and microcomputer repair training, we found that participants needed roughly ninth grade reading and math levels, as well as some background in electronics. More than half of the applicants failed the entrance exams, a fact that indicated reading and math scores below these levels.

Our experiences are by no means unusual. In inner cities throughout the country, at least half of inner city young people, 16-21 years of age have reading and math skills below the eighth grade. This is the literacy level needed for many entry level jobs in urban labor markets. Further, it is the level needed for most of the skills training, not only business machine repair and microcomputer repair, but also word processing, drafting, and data entry training.

Part of the inner city illiteracy is due to the continued high dropout rate. Nationwide, an estimated 27% of students fail to complete their high school education, up from 23% in 1974. [1] Dropout rates are highest for minorities and in major cities. In 1980, among those 15-19 years of age, an estimated 15% of whites, 21% of blacks, and 39% of Hispanics, were not enrolled in school and did not have a high school diploma. [2] Among major cities, New York and Chicago had dropout rates in 1984 estimated at 45% and 55% respectively. [3]

Low literacy rates, though, are by no means limited to the dropout rolls. High school seniors are graduating with fifth and sixth grade reading and math levels. Nationwide, the most complete study of illiteracy was done by the National Assessment of Educational Progress (NAEP) in 1975. Unlike the Census Bureau estimates of illiteracy, which measure illiteracy solely on the basis of schooling, NAEP estimates are based on reading materials selected as "frequently encountered in everyday life" and necessary for functioning in both the job and the social mainstream. Questions sought to identify the abilities to understand word meaning, to glean significant facts, to comprehend the main idea and organization in paragraphs. Samples included:

- A replica of a "help wanted" advertisement that required identification of starting and quitting times, minimum age, and how to apply locally;
- A book club membership application asking for the amount of money to be sent with the application;
- A report card asking on which subject the recipient was improving.

The designers of the test set a level of 75% of correct answers as the minimum needed to be considered functionally literate. By this standard, 12.6% of all 17 year olds enrolled in school in the United States were defined as functionally illiterate, with 44.4% defined as semi-illiterate (missing more than 10% of questions but less than 25%). Among blacks, though, the corresponding figures were 41.6% functionally illiterate and 82.7% semi-literate[4]. Another major study, the Armed Services Vocational Aptitude Battery, was administered to a nationally representative sample of 18-23 year olds in 1980. The median reading score for the nation was 9.6 grade level. Of the total,

18% had reading scores below the seventh grade, and the median reading scores for blacks and Hispanics were 6.8 and 7.5 respectively.[5]

The Oakland Public School District is an urban district with a heavy minority enrollment: 64% black and 11% Hispanic. In 1984 the Oakland School Board commissioned a study of the schools by Professor James Guthrie of U.C. Berkeley. Guthrie found that in five of the six Oakland high schools, the average senior was scoring at a ninth grade level in math and English, fully three years behind the national average.[6]

Why is this so? Why are more than half of our inner city high school seniors unable to read with comprehension or unable to understand percentages? It is a question we asked often at Renaissance and discussed among our students. The home environment repeatedly was singled out. The students themselves talked of the lack of encouragement from the home. Books are not a regular part of the household environment, and academic study does not have a high priority. Beyond the home, there is the lack of prestige that academic study carries throughout the neighborhood. Academic achievement is not seen as leading anywhere, is not connected to employment or opportunities.

In the schools the inner city youth may be promoted grade after grade even if skills are not acquired. The teacher receives little support for holding back a student who fails to progress adequately. In fact, to do so is only to risk complaint from the student, and perhaps the parents. On the other side, rarely is there any reward for the teacher who does make outstanding progress with students.

Yet, though the public schools are not reaching many inner city teen-agers, there are literacy upgrading programs operated by job training agencies outside the schools that are doing so. These programs, operating quietly, are improving math and reading scores one and two grade levels in three-month periods. They are aiding high school dropouts to obtain degrees, and aiding previously semi-literate dropouts and semi-literate high school graduates into the job mainstream.

I first came into contact with one of these programs in 1980, when Renaissance still was a volunteer organization. My contact was through Rodger Scott, who taught in Project Excel, a literacy course sponsored by the job training organization Youth for Service. Rodger spent a lot of unpaid time tutoring students in the class, and I was impressed by his dedication.

There were high school dropouts coming to Renaissance who clearly were bright. They had been out in the labor market for a time, been rejected for jobs, and had come to understand the need for a high school diploma. A few were persuaded to give Project Excel a try. The results were striking. Carlos Bustamonte improved reading scores by two grade levels within a three-month period and obtained the high school diploma. Alex Young improved both reading and math scores three grade levels within three months. He too obtained a high school diploma.

Project Excel had three features that distinguished it from the public schools. First, there was an intensiveness. The course extended only three hours a day. But during those hours the focus was on math and reading. There was no division into different periods—history, physical education, art—and no electives.

Second, the instructor was accountable for student success. Continued financing of the program was based on continued student gains. At the same time, the instructor, Rodger Scott, was dedicated to the program beyond the money: he often volunteered time after class to work with students, and the students recognized his concern.

Third and perhaps most important, instruction was connected to the specific goal of the high school diploma. It was a goal that could be reached in three months or less. It was a goal also linked to the main student goal of employment.

In all, 10 of the 15 students in Project Excel achieved the high school diploma.

At Renaissance we decided to launch a literacy class in response to the very low reading and math levels of applicants to our skills training courses. Many of these applicants had strong motivation to go into the technician trades and good mechanical skills, though their reading and/or math was below eighth grade.

The class, termed Tech Prep, was designed to work with applicants at the sixth and seventh grade levels and improve their skills to the needed eighth and ninth grades. It was to include high school dropouts as well as high school graduates. It was to be four months in length. It was to lead participants either into our technician training, to other advanced vocational training (phototypesetting, word processing), or directly into jobs.

We recruited through flyers, radio advertisements and word of mouth. One-fourth or so of the applicants decided against taking the course when they learned that we would not be paying training stipends. Under CETA, many literacy courses paid students $3.35 per hour to attend class, and youth had grown accustomed to this.

Nonetheless, we had more than enough applicants and enrolled 17 students. The main incentive was the advanced training or job. We told students, "If you go through this course seriously and steadily, we'll make sure you get into technician training or a job." We drew up contracts, by which, in return, students agreed to "attend every class and be on time," "work and participate to the best of my ability and try," and "keep a positive attitude."

During the next three months, 4 students dropped out of class. The remaining 13 completed, with most registering impressive progress.

Of these 13 students 6 were high school graduates and 7 were high school dropouts. There was a striking contrast between the graduates and dropouts. Almost without exception, the dropouts entered Tech Prep with better reading and writing skills than the graduates.

Three of the 6 high school graduates were below the sixth grade levels when they entered. On their applications, they wrote the following answers to the question asking for a paragraph on personal goals:

"To own my own business. In a nightclob and to get my license."

"My interest are finding a good job to support myself and my goal is to get a job in the field I'm working which is business so that I maybe able to help others find what they want out of life but I must help myself first."

"My goals in life are to receiving the training in the field of computer science."

In contrast, the answers by the high school dropouts were more complete and had fewer misspellings. Examples included,

"I want to get my diploma and then maybe go to college. I'll also get a part-time job. I want a job that is very interesting not routine because I like different situations."

"My current interest and goal in life is to obtain a successful and interesting job that is well paid as well as interesting."

The course consisted of two hours of reading and writing and an hour of math. The traditional instruction was complemented by the use of microcomputers. Students quickly mastered the computers and used a variety of education programs, practicing reading comprehension and basic math. The computers possessed a glamour, and students stayed after class to work on them. The class also included instruction in job search skills—how to write a resume, how to locate job openings, how to interview—as well as discussions about the work environment.

6 of the 7 high school dropouts did obtain a diploma, by passing a battery of exams known as the GED. They registered gains not only in reading and math and the use of computers, but also in writing, logic, and intellectual confidence—all qualities integral to longer term labor market success. The process of getting the high school diploma itself provided a big boost in confidence. At the conclusion of the class, four continued in Renaissance technician training, one entered City College, and one started a job.

Of the 6 high school graduates, three continued in Renaissance technician training, one went on to engineering training, and two started jobs. On the tests of Adult Basic Education, they showed gains in both vocabulary and comprehension of one to three years. Even more telling than their showing on these limited-range official tests (which were multiple choice), was their ability to take tests (a significant skill in job searches) and their ability to start composing essays. The student who wrote, "To own my own business. Buy a nightclob and get my fcc license" as his statement of goals continued through the first month of the course unable to write more than a sentence on any topic. By the end of the course, he was able to write two or three paragraphs on a subject. To be sure, these paragraphs were riddled with misspellings and grammatical mistakes ("I think that school shood have a better learning system and better teachers"), but he had the beginnings of the skills he needed. He had started to learn to organize thoughts into a coherent presentation. He would continue writing practice as he entered the office machine technician training.

Indeed, for all of the students, the three month period was not sufficient to improve reading and especially writing skills to the level needed for most business correspondence or business transactions. Whether they would gain these skills depended on their perseverance in learning. The class, though, had prepared them for advanced vocational training and for some entry-level jobs. As important, it had set in motion intellectual generators and abilities that had long stood idle. For years, most of these young men and women had not seriously exercised reading and logic abilities.

The ability of the course to reach students not reached by the public schools was due to some of the same factors that explain the success of Project Excel. The instructor was closely accountable for student gains. The instruction was intensive. Most of all, the instruction was connected to the specific goals of the GED and/or advanced vocational training or jobs. Students could see the training as leading somewhere.

Further, the literacy instruction benefited from the use of the students' experiences in the instruction and from the use of computers. The Tech Prep director, Martha Williams, had found over years of teaching high school dropouts that many simply couldn't understand writing assignments at school. The subject matter often was too abstract or distant from their experiences. Thus, she came to use course materials that were more connected to these experiences. For example, the students might read an essay about "common sense" versus "college education". This would be followed by a discussion of different types of education. After ideas had been put forward and listed on the blackboard, the students would be asked to write a one-page essay. The exercise was designed not to teach theories of education but (taking a subject that touched upon the students) to practice analyzing a subject, developing ideas, and articulating these ideas on paper.

The computers were a valuable teaching adjunct. They had a glamour to them; they had a mystery and future to them that attracted students. Also, the computers enabled students to proceed at their own pace and to make corrections without embarrassment.

Tech Prep has become a regular part of Renaissance training. In addition, across the country, other community groups also are giving greater attention to literacy instruction and are showing similar educational gains.

A major Ford Foundation effort currently is being made through the Remediation and Training Center of Washington, D.C. The center has developed a computer-based literacy program focused on basic skills improvement. Initial results show improvements in reading comprehension and vocabulary ranging from one and a half to two grades for every 100 hours of training.

The center was established in 1982 principally by Robert Taggart, who served in the Department of Labor as head of youth employment programs during the Carter administration. Taggart had spent much of the previous decade researching and writing about various types of skills training and on-the-job training programs. He came to see this training as missing the major employment barrier facing inner city young people: the lack of basic reading and writing skills. From research in job training, he was led into research on the teaching of basic skills. A similar path was taken by another official of the Department of Labor, Gordon Berlin. Berlin was struck by the role in most job hiring of basic skills and work orientation, rather than specific skills. After leaving the department in 1981, he came to the Ford Foundation and joined with Taggart in researching a variety of basic skills programs in the military and Job Corps, voluntary tutoring programs, and Adult Basic Education programs. They found that a number of these programs were experiencing dramatic literacy gains as they emphasized self-paced forms of instruction—requiring successful completion of one lesson or competency unit before moving to the next—and as they linked literacy to job training or work experience that required the use of new skills.

Berlin and Taggart developed a training curriculum and in 1984 began to test it at community groups across the nation. Initial results show the average gains of one and a half to two years for every 100 hours of training.[7] Barbara Johnson, a training director at the Remediation and Training Center, attributes the gains to the intensiveness of the training—three hours a day of focused training—the self-paced approach, and accompanying use of computers.

In their writing on community-based literacy programs, Berlin and Taggart emphasize that gains are likely to decay unless they are followed by job training or jobs that make use of the skills. This is a main reason why they are working with community groups that are oriented to job placement.

Also, they point out that the most serious obstacle encountered in the basic literacy classes "is keeping students engaged long enough to achieve the desired gains." Nearly all of the students are restless to make money. On one level, they see the need to "better themselves," to better their skills for getting a "good job." But this long-term perspective often is over-whelmed by a shorter-term perspective to make money now. Even more than vocational courses, Berlin and Taggart have found, literacy courses are undermined by dropouts who hold a day-to-day perspective.[8]

Indeed, for all of the successes of Tech Prep and Project Excel, both have suffered over the longer run from dropout rates averaging over 25 percent. At Renaissance we thought that dropping out could be reduced through part-time jobs. Students would work in the afternoon, earn money, and see in the work setting the importance of literacy. In practice, though, half of the Tech Prep students who obtained part-time jobs stopped coming to class, preferring to make money.

An inability to remain long in class was most serious precise-ly among the unemployed adults who came to Renaissance with the lowest reading levels—those reading at below the seventh grade level.

Flushed with the success of Tech Prep, Renaissance joined with two other inner city training organizations, the Ella Hill Hutch Community Center in the Fillmore district and Young Community Developers in Hunters Point, to launch Literacy Upgrading for Career Development (LUCD) in June 1985. LUCD focused on unemployed adults with the lowest reading level, below seventh grade. There was great excitement about LUCD, for all three organizations saw it as a means of reaching the hard-core unemployed, who were not reached by other train-ing programs.

At this time, inner city illiteracy was beginning to be dis-covered as an "issue" by the national press. Jonathan Kozol's book *Illiterate America* had attracted attention, and articles appeared reciting the low performance of inner city young people on the national reading and math tests. The San Francisco Private Industry Council entered into a $150,000 contract with LUCD to train 50 unemployed adults with severe reading deficiencies. The program goal was to raise reading scores at least two to three grades years within an eighth month period.

The $150,000 contract was far more money than Renaissance had seen in its previous literacy efforts, and it enabled each class to be staffed generously with an instructor, a tutor, and a counselor. When these positions were announced, LUCD received hundreds of applicants, and we were able to choose teachers and counselors with years of experience.

All of the elements were in place for success. Reuben Thomas, a counselor, recruited at the welfare office and housing projects, telling potential participants, "This is an opportunity to improve your reading skills, even to obtain a high school diploma. With better skills you'll be able to obtain better jobs, to move up from the fast-food jobs that you're looking at now." For the first training cycle, 25 participants were enrolled.

By the third month, fewer than one-half of the participants were attending class on a steady basis. By the conclusion of the first training cycle at eight months, only one-third of the participants had made significant reading and/or employment gains. Upon admission to the program, each claimed that he or she was dedicated to improving basic skills and would stick with the training. However, by the third month, these participants usually became restless and dropped out to find a job. "Stay in class, invest in your future, be able to compete for better jobs," the counselors would tell them, "If you leave now, you will get only fast-food jobs." But these exhortations did little to halt the dropout rate. Each week I met with the two other executive directors, Leonard "Lefty" Gordon of the Ella Hill Hutch Community Center and Cleo Rand of Young Community Developers, to discuss ways of improving attendance, which had sunk to six or seven students per day. One week we decided to try a stricter screening process for admission. Another week, we set a more formal student review process. Still another week, we decided to emphasize part-time jobs. Each of these methods did little to halt the dropout rate.

Among the one-third or so of students who did attend regularly, some of the same dramatic educational and motivational gains were achieved as in Tech Prep. Ginna Hunter, 28, was on welfare and "bored at home" when she enrolled, after failing the entrance exam for Renaissance's microcomputer repair course. Her attendance was nearly perfect, for, as she explained at the graduation ceremony, "It was the first time I saw myself succeeding." She went on to training as a licensed vocational nurse. Marcus Mabry, 19, earned his high school diploma and a job with a security firm. His explanation: "I proved I could complete something."

But more typical of the students, especially the young men, was James McFarland. McFarland, 20, entered the program with a high school diploma but a reading level between the sixth and seventh grade. "I know I need to improve my reading for a better job," he said at the entrance interview, adding that he did not want a life of fast-food jobs. After a few weeks his attendance became irregular, and he told the counselor, Reuben Thomas, that he wanted to work. Reuben helped him to land a part-time job at a downtown restaurant. Still, his attendance faltered, and he dropped out to seek a full-time job— though when Reuben saw him four months later, he had not found one. "I wish I knew how to reach James," said Reuben. "On one level, he wants to improve skills, but on another level..."

After its first one-year contract ended, LUCD was given a one-year extension, contingent upon improved participant retention and achievement. Lefty Gordon, chaired the LUCD management council, and he pushed for this contingency arrangement. With government training funds so limited, LUCD could be justified only if class size averaged at least 12-13 students per day.

Lefty, though, was not about to give up on LUCD or the possibilities of reaching the lowest-level readers. His view: With all of LUCD's disappointments, it still was able to spur achievement out of many young inner city women and men who had not been reached by the public schools. Further, it was doing so at a lower cost per student than the public schools.

For me, LUCD was clear indication that literacy upgrading among the lowest level readers was more complex than the "more government compassion and money" view of Jonathan Kozol and the other new literacy prophets. LUCD was sufficiently funded; other changes were needed to improve participant retention.

However, it was also clear to me that the community-based literacy program with a job nexus was the approach of greatest promise in reducing inner city illiteracy. Project Excel, Tech Prep, the Remediation and Training Center, and even to an extent LUCD, were tapping inner city talent and abilities not tapped by the public schools, with a fraction of the resources of the public schools.

My belief in the promise of these literacy classes was strengthened as I remained in touch with students and saw gains continue.

Anna Burgos was a student in the first Tech Prep class. She was 19 when she came to Renaissance, and had dropped out of Mission High School two years earlier. In a story heard over and over at Renaissance, she knew that she should get a high school diploma, but found classes boring and leading nowhere. Her friends were skipping classes, and she began to do so. One day, she just stopped going altogether. Nobody at the school seemed to notice, or said anything. Nor did her mother seek to persuade her to continue. The next year, she made another attempt to start classes at Mission but left after a few weeks.

In the summer of 1984 she signed up for the federal summer jobs program, to get a job and make money. From this program she heard of Tech Prep, as an opportunity to go to school part-time and work part-time.

At the start, her attendance was irregular. But as the class proceeded, she blossomed. She came regularly, she participated in class discussions, she became friends with other class members. She passed the battery of GED exams and the entrance exam for microcomputer repair. Near the end of the course, she wrote the following essay reflecting on the class:

When I started the tech-prep class, I knew it would be a great opportunity for me and the time was also just right. I had just failed to graduate for the second time and the class gave me a chance not only to get my GED but also training in the field microcomputer repair. It was something I was interested in and a chance I couldn't pass up. Anyway I didn't want to go back to high school.

Well now it's two months later and I'm a week away from taking the entrance exam to the microcomputer class. I passed my GED and feel good about how things are going. I met a lot of people who are now my friends and I enjoy being in the same class with them.

In organization, grammar, and spelling, the essay is far above most of the writing by inner city young people who come to Renaissance, and Anna's essay was one of the top two or three papers in the class. Its quality was not solely or even mainly the result of the three months of Tech Prep; Anna clearly brought far more talent and intelligence to the class than most students. Tech Prep started to tap this talent and intelligence.

After Tech Prep Anna went on to the microcomputer repair class. She completed it, but was turned down by each of the first five electronics companies she applied to. When the Tech Prep director, Marty Williams, followed up with calls to these companies, she was told that despite Anna's training, other applicants with years of high school and even college training possessed greater skills.

Anna gave up looking for jobs and for a time seemed to lapse into a routine of staying at home and watching television and drinking. But Marty continued to set job interviews and push Anna to try. On Anna's eleventh interview, she was hired by Computerland, whose personnel chief was one of the first graduates of the Renaissance microcomputer training. At this writing, nine months later, Anna continues to work at Computerland.

NOTES — Reading and Writing below the Ninth Grade Level

1. U.S. Department of Education, "Fact Sheet on Nationwide Functional Literacy Initiative," Washington, D.C., 1983.

2. Ernest Boyer, *High School: A Report on Secondary Education in America*, New York, Harper & Row, 1983.

3. Gordon Berlin, "Education, Equity, and Economic Excellence," New York, Ford Foundation, 1984.

4. Charles Gadway, *Right to Read: Functional Literacy*, Denver, National Assessment of Educational Progress, 1976.

5. Profile of American Youth, "1980 Nationwide Administration of the Armed Services Vocational Aptitude Battery," Washington, D.C., Office of the Assistant Secretary of Defense, 1982.

6. James Guthrie, "Schooling in Oakland: The Challenge," Berkeley, University of California, Berkeley, School of Education 1985.

7. Robert Taggart, "Questions and Answers about the Comprehensive Competencies Program," Alexandria, VA, Remediation and Training Institute, 1984.

8. Gordon Berlin, *Not Working: Unskilled Youth and Displaced Adults*, New York, Ford Foundation, 1983; Gordon Berlin, "Education, Equity and Economic Excellence: The Critical Role of Second Chance Basic Skills and Job Training Programs," New York, Ford Foundation, 1984.

Chapter 5

Unemployment and the Inner Compass

"I went to the Urban League office, but Mr. Steve Martin—that's his name—wasn't there. Then you know, Mike, I went to Ticketron to apply for a job, but they weren't taking applications. My friend said that she heard about a job at a shoe store in Daly City, and she's going to give me an address."

Louise Allen was talking about her job search over the past week, but no longer was I listening. Each week for the past three months, she had stopped by Renaissance, wanting to borrow a few dollars to supplement her welfare check, and talking about her desire to find a job. Yet, though she said she wanted a job, her actions undermined steady work. She missed appointments, dropped out of a training program, disappeared to Los Angeles for a week. Her scattered actions bore the characteristic I had come to see in too many of the unemployed coming to Renaissance: the lack of an inner compass, oriented to the steady work world.

Youth from all economic backgrounds move around the labor market and change jobs often. This movement can be beneficial, as it provides a sample of opportunities. But the job instability of Louise and also of her ex-husband Walter bore more disturbing elements: a lack of job and social attachments, and (in Louise's case) an acceptance of welfare support.

When I first met Louise in 1980, I was certain that she would succeed in the labor market. Renaissance at the time was a volunteer network of business and labor persons helping the unemployed find jobs on a one-to-one basis. Louise had been referred by her boyfriend, Walter Allen, who had come to Renaissance a few months earlier. Louise's two sisters were on welfare, but she declared, "I'm never going to be on welfare; I'm going to make something of my life."

Louise was 18, and recently graduated from Lincoln High School. She was looking for a clerical job and noted that she could type over 50 words a minute. She had a pleasant, soft-spoken personality and a neat appearance.

The clerical position is the one non professional position in the Bay Area in which demand far exceeds supply. "A good secretary" is the job nearly always cited by personnel officials in need of applicants. Louise would be far easier to place into a job than many of the young men, who preferred the very scarce craft or construction jobs.

Within a month, Louise was hired by a major insurance company to be a clerk typist. The job was not glamorous: it involved typing hundreds of the same insurance forms. But Louise exclaimed, "I can't wait to get started." The office was in the Alcoa Building, overlooking the Bay, and it promised a steady paycheck.

From the first day, though, her supervisor seemed to criticize everything she did. She wasn't fast enough in typing forms. She made too many typing mistakes. On the third day of the job, she was fired.

"Don't get down. You'll get another job," Walter tried to comfort her. Louise had the talent and skills and could easily get another job. A businessman in the Renaissance network gave her a series of job leads. Instead of moving forward, she withdrew. She went to live with her sister and made only halfhearted attempts to find work. Walter was not surprised, commenting, "Louise will go off and do crazy things."

Indeed, as I later learned, Louise had been in and out of a few jobs when she came to Renaissance. She did graduate from Lincoln High and had entered City College. Within two months, though, she began dating Marcus, a young man who worked as a stock clerk and an assistant preacher at a small fundamentalist church. He persuaded her to leave school and marry him. They moved into a $370 a month apartment in Civic Center, though it was far above his income.

Louise obtained a job as a clerk typist at Bank of America, working 8:00 A.M.-5:00 P.M. She also participated in the church activities. She attended services and bible classes until 1:00 A.M. Soon she was coming late for work, first at 8:30 then at 9:00. She knew she should be on time, but she couldn't seem to wake up. Even after her supervisor put her on notice, she came late. A few weeks later, she was fired.

Soon Louise grew disillusioned with both Marcus and the church. Marcus also had lost his job and was spending all his time at the church. The main preacher, a barber, had closed his barbershop and was living on church donations. By May she separated from Marcus, went to live with her sister, and took up with Walter.

Prodded by Walter, Louise did resume her job search three months after being fired by the insurance company. She found a typist job at Ticketron but was laid off in two months. She found a job as a film developer that paid $4.50 an hour but left after a month, deciding that she missed clerical work.

She contacted major banks, Wells Fargo, Crocker, Bank of America, and completed applications. She did pass the typing speed exams but failed each time on the spelling and grammar. Her spelling skills were rated at the fifth grade, despite her high school graduation.

Before she could find a job, she discovered she was pregnant with Walter's child. Encouraged by her sisters, she joined the welfare rolls. Her sister was evicted for not paying rent, so Louise went to live with her aunt in Hunters Point. She slept in the living room, which meant that she usually didn't sleep until one or two in the morning. She would have continued this life on welfare, though, except that her aunt was receiving welfare, and Louise thought she could not use her aunt's address. After her welfare checks stopped coming to her sister's old address, she found herself off the welfare rolls.

Getting off welfare galvanized her into action. She immediately looked for work. She checked with the private employment agencies and was sent to three temporary clerical assignments. She worked until nearly a month before she gave birth to a daughter, Capricia Marie Allen. Three months later, she married Walter. At this time, Louise stopped by Renaissance to say that she would be looking for work soon. She brought a picture showing her and Walter proudly holding Capricia.

Louise returned to the employment agencies and was able to obtain assignments. But now she had a new difficulty, day care for Capricia. She tried leaving her with Walter's sister Belinda, who lived in a nearby housing project, and who had two children of her own. Belinda was unreliable. Without notice, she would announce in the morning that she had to take her children to the doctor or had to cash her welfare check. Twice Louise called the employment agency to say she couldn't continue on a job, and on another occasion she left the office early. This last occasion was painful for the assignment was at Itel, an office that she enjoyed and that offered the possibility of permanent work. A woman who lived two doors down from her offered to take care of Capricia for $5.00 a day. This woman, though, soon proved as unreliable as Belinda.

Louise went back on welfare for a few months and then suddenly appeared at Renaissance. By now, Renaissance had a small full-time staff, and an interview was arranged with a law firm seeking a file clerk. Louise got the job. For a time, the child care was handled by a neighbor, who charged only $4.00 a day.

This time, though, Louise was fired after three months, not for her inability to come on time, but for her inability to handle the filing. A file was lost. The file was needed by a senior partner in the firm, and Louise was held responsible. Louise claimed the lost file wasn't her fault, but for the supervisor of the filing department, the lost file was one more mistake by Louise. "We can't run a training program here," the supervisor told Renaissance.

At this time, fall 1982, Louise not only was back on welfare, but also had separated from Walter and returned to live with her aunt. Louise complained that Walter "mistreated" her. Walter complained that Louise didn't want to work and preferred to receive Aid to Families with Dependent Children (AFDC) ("just like her sisters"), and he wasn't going to be dragged down by her.

Over the next two years, we at Renaissance saw Louise only sporadically. A Renaissance counselor helped her find a receptionist job at the San Francisco Bar Association. Again, this job lasted less than four months. "We all found Louise pleasant and willing to work," the bar personnel chief explained, "but she missed so many days and seemed to have so many personal problems that we had to let her go. Her former husband, Walter, would stop by or call, and they would argue."

After this job, Louise settled onto AFDC. I didn't see her until she appeared out of the blue at Renaissance in 1985. She had moved into one of the cheap residential hotels on Valencia Street, a few doors down from us. Though she retained her pleasant, youthful manner, her neat appearance had become a disheveled, disorganized look. Her red nail polish was chipping, and she wore the top of a jogging suit that was a size too small. She said that she had come to look for work and added that her welfare check was late and could she borrow five dollars?

In the first months of Renaissance, we had loaned money to participants, but this practice quickly ended when most of the money was not repaid. Yet, Louise never had asked for money in the past, and I did not think twice about advancing five dollars.

"I know I've messed up in the past, but now it's a different story," she continued. "I'm going to get off welfare, do good." Down the street from Renaissance was Arriba Juntos, a community group that offered a short brush-up class for clerical training and job placement. That would be the best step for Louise; and she agreed to enroll. The next week, she started class.

"Louise isn't ready to enroll in training," the program director at Arriba Juntos called to tell me two weeks later. "She came late three days the first week and missed two days this week." Louise had been dropped from the training program and told to come back when she was serious about training. Louise said she lost her alarm clock.

Over the next two months, Louise stopped by at Renaissance once or twice a week. Usually she would start by describing this or that place she visited and put in an application for employment and then, by the way, ask if she could borrow three or four dollars. The sums always were modest, and always accompanied by an explanation that her welfare check was late and she would pay Renaissance back on the first or the fifteenth of the month.

One Monday morning she called from Los Angeles to say that she was in the Greyhound bus station and had no money and asked if we could wire her $45 to get back to San Francisco. In the background, I could hear Capricia crying and the bus schedules being announced. What was she doing at the Greyhound bus station? "I don't know, it was a crazy thing to do."

"We can't always keep bailing her out of problems," was Don's reaction. "She's come to use us as a crutch." I feared this was the case and took no action, to see how she would make do on her own. But she kept calling throughout the day, and the next. On Tuesday afternoon I asked Cleland House, a community group in East Los Angeles sponsoring a project with Renaissance, to forward the money. She arrived back in San Francisco the next day.

It was difficult to be mad at Louise. Her life had been so wretched. Her father left the family before she was born, and she grew up in a series of foster homes. Louise last saw her mother when she was twelve and thought that her mother had been in and out of jail on prostitution and robbery charges in the years since. Her sisters were on welfare and a brother in prison. Now Louise, barely more than a kid herself, had a four-year-old child to raise alone. She lived in a one-room apartment in a building filled with drug addicts and violent men.

Yet, however wretched her life, clearly none of the "compassionate" liberal approaches of welfare or job training really was helping her. The welfare grant she received was meager: $474 a month plus food stamps of $60 a month. Yet, as long as she received welfare with no expectations, her work incentive was limited. I gave her a few dollars from time to time and encouraged her to enroll in a clerical training program, but this encouragement largely fell on deaf ears.

Walter Allen too had encountered difficulty in the job market since 1980, when he appeared so fresh and ready to work.

"I just got your letter this morning. Can I come in this afternoon for a job?" Walter asked. It was the fall of 1980, and Walter, 20 years old, recently had returned from a year and a half in the Job Corps. Job Corps' officials had asked me to contact Walter to help with his job search. As a volunteer, I had offered job assistance at this time to more than 50 Job Corps graduates, but none had seemed as excited about working as Walter or was as quick to call me.

We did meet later that same afternoon. He had achieved his high school diploma through the Job Corps. Also at the corps, he had specialized in tile laying and painting and received a certificate for outstanding achievement as a painter. In June 1980 he returned to San Francisco, looking forward to a full time job as a painter.

He did not find a job as a painter. At the painters' union hall, he was told of a long waiting list for union membership. Even many of the current union members were without steady work.

He next checked with two agencies funded by the federal government specifically to help minority young people into apprenticeships: the Apprenticeship Opportunities Foundation and the
San Francisco Skills Bank. Both asked him to complete an application, for their service records, but neither offered job possibilities. For apprenticeships in plumbing and electrical wiring,
for example, the job lists opened only once every year or two. For
apprenticeships in carpentry and painting, applicants needed
to contact contractors directly. Neither agency offered leads to
contractors. Walter made three calls to contractors and gave up.
The Christmas season was coming, and I suggested that Walter
contact the department stores in San Francisco, which hired
temporary stock clerks. Walter was hired by Macy's at $4.75 an
hour to do stock work. "This is my big break," he announced.

Walter worked at the job for four weeks and then was fired.
His explanation was that his supervisor disliked him, yelled at
him. The supervisor said that Walter took too long coffee breaks
and had cursed him and the store during his termination interview.

Walter did not give up. Within a month he found a job as a
dishwasher at Scott's, a prominent seafood restaurant. The pay
was only $3.35 an hour, but Walter expressed determination to
work hard and move up. After three months he applied to advance to a busboy position at Scott's, and was disappointed when
the restaurant hired from outside ("They say they promote from
within, and then they go out and do this"). Still, he stayed with
the job, moving up to $3.60 an hour after eight months.

In October 1981, he was hired in stock work at a drapery factory. The pay was higher, at $4.65 an hour, and the job involved
greater diversity of tasks. This time, though, the job ended after
three weeks when the factory closed.

Again, Walter did not give up. Hearing that janitorial work paid $7-$9 an hour in San Francisco, he applied to janitorial companies. At the Moscone Convention Center he found two friends on the cleanup crew, who told him the job paid $7.50 an hour. When the foreman questioned whether Walter had experience, Walter asked to be given a chance to prove himself. The foreman called the next day to say there were six people ahead of Walter, but he would keep Walter's application.

Walter grew discouraged during the next weeks, as his mother pressured him to look harder. "I was feeling real bad about not finding something. My mother thought I was just laying up. You know I'd do it so many days a week and then I'd wait and rest to hear from some people. She kept telling me, "Well, I'll be glad when you get a job and she kept worrying, thinking I wasn't going to start looking and things like that." Then, on a Friday afternoon three weeks later, the foreman called Walter to say he was laying off two men, and to ask if Walter wanted a job. Walter started work the next Monday.

The job started sometimes at seven in the morning and sometimes at three in the afternoon, but Walter was careful to be on time, to keep the job. During a crew meeting in the third month, Walter thought he had lost the job when the foreman singled him out. Instead the foreman praised him for his "good attitude." A few days earlier, Walter had told an older white man in a suit that he enjoyed the cleanup crew and seeing the place in order. The man was the head of the convention center, and he congratulated the foreman.

By June 1982, the sixth month on the job, Walter's future with the job seemed secure. He talked of going to school at night and learning a skill, probably computers. He talked of getting an apartment, maybe buying a house.

Up to this point, for the previous one and a half years, I had spoken with Wayne weekly. Now, with many more young people coming to Renaissance and with Walter secure in a job, we talked less, and I saw him infrequently. Over the next year, I heard reports that he and Louise had separated, but I did not hear from him directly until August 1983, when he was arrested for carrying a concealed weapon. Louise had called the police when she heard him approach her aunt's apartment and call to speak with her. The police found a gun concealed in Walter's car.

Walter was given probation on this charge, but a short time later, he called to say he had been fired from his job for fighting.

I was setting up at Civic Center, when this guy, a friend of Louise comes up and tries to start a fight. He says, "Aren't you the one who's been talking all this shit about Louise", and I said, "Well I don't want to get into a fight now". But then he gets me into a chokehold, and starts slamming me against the wall, so I hit him. Then the foreman comes and says "Well you know our policy, the one who throws the first punch is guilty,"so l was fired.

The union tried to prevent his firing and later helped him find another job as a freight elevator operator. This new job paid even better, $10.65 an hour. Walter worked for nearly a year on this job, until the elevator system was automated and the job was eliminated. After this job ended, Walter did not follow his previous procedures and rush to get a new job. Instead, he drew unemployment insurance and "kicked back" for a time. Despite the good wage of his job, he had not saved any money. The state claimed that he owed $1,200 in delinquent child support payments.

During the year he worked as a freight elevator operator, Walter had two brushes with the law. In one case, he was sitting in a downtown restaurant when a middle aged man pointed Walter out to police as the robber who tried to steal his wallet a few hours earlier in a downtown parking lot. Walter was arrested but released. Charges were dropped when the man decided not to go through with prosecution. Then six months later, Walter was arrested for a street robbery. This time he pleaded guilty in return for probation.

Now, while he collected unemployment benefits, Walter was arrested for pickpocket activity on the crowded 38 Geary bus. This time he served two months in the county jail, with sentence suspended unless he was arrested within three months.

Two months passed, during which period he remained unemployed and not really looking for work. Then he was arrested again on charges of grand theft. This time, he was charged with using force to steal a man's handbag in the downtown area, near Post and Powell.

I heard about these incidents from a Renaissance participant, recently released from the temporary county jail at 850 Bryant. A few days later, I drove to the main San Francisco county jail in San Bruno to see Walter.

"When they came and told me I had a visitor, I didn't know who to expect. You're the first person who's come," said Walter as we shook hands in the jail's "conversation room." He was dressed in the standard orange jumpsuit, but he otherwise appeared as healthy and neat in appearance as when we first met. "I bet you never thought I'd end up in here," he added. "I sure didn't".

He talked of his most recent arrest and his plea-bargain, two days earlier, to a year in prison. He minimized the robbery, saying he had used no force, but did not try to argue his innocence. He pointed to drugs as the cause of his actions. "The drugs, you know, they eased my mind, and before long I didn't care about anything else." He was resigned to spending time in prison but still saw a future for himself. "I want to go back to school, get a trade for myself. Probably computers, I mean fixing or operating computers." He didn't want anything to do with Louise ("She's so mixed up, I never should have got with her") but did plan to see his daughter Capricia, whom he hadn't seen in two years.

As I was leaving, he asked whether I might help him get a job when he applied for the work furlough program. He also asked whether he might call collect from time to time, as he had "no one else on the outside." As I drove home from the jail, I tried to think of job training approaches that might have been more successful with Walter. Looked at individually, a number of his job disappointments (in painting, the drapery factory) were beyond his control. However, taken together, they show a disturbing pattern in Walter's inability to work steadily in a low-level job and advance. Neither the formal Job Corps training nor the informal Renaissance job counseling had led Walter to a strong or continued success in jobs. I thought that after serving time in prison, he would find this success: he did not show the deep antisocial behavior of other incarcerated young people. But could not his transition to work have been less lengthy and costly to himself and society?

The Job Corps seemingly had been effective: he did obtain a GED and learn a trade during the year and a half. However, the GED turned out to be little more than paper. He still read and wrote at a sixth grade level. This I discovered when he had to write a description of himself for the probation department in 1983. It read in part:

Life history I was born and Lasouesia. 11-16-60. My mother name is Marion Allen. Her maiden was Marion Reed. She is 46 yrs old now. My brother name's is Mieahle, Regenled and Leslie Jr. I half one sister. Her Name is Belinda Gaffeny Employment history My fruist job was a summer job at downtown high as a jaintor my type of work was buffing waking mopping. The pay at that time was $3.35 an hrs, My 2 job was at Scotty Seafood Their I was a dashwasher makeking $3.60 an hr. I quited to fined better at ABC Draprie factor Their I was makeing $4.75 hr.

Marital History: I am married right now but separated The reason why is because she dindt like to work She is now receiveing A.f.d.c. to support my baby an Im paying child support of $1.50 a month an this is my furits time married. Her maiden name is Lousie Walliam. She is 22 yrs old now. My marrier was a waste of my time.

With these poor verbal skills, Walter can get many jobs, even well- paying jobs, in the Bay Area. However, many of the careers are closed to him, including computers. Despite his talk of "getting into computers," he could not last a week in a computer technician class. At the same time, it is difficult to blame the Job Corps. After reading Walter's report, Don encouraged him to improve his writing skills, to take a class at Renaissance or at night at community college, both free of cost. Walter talked about taking a class but never followed through.

Louise similarly never followed through on training classes available. With her, though, a lack of work motivation was related to welfare. Welfare placed no expectations on her, and she seemed to have given up on herself. Only when welfare was cut off did she spring into action and find jobs.

In the months after Louise's Greyhound bus episode and my visit with Walter in jail—both occurred around the same time— I thought increasingly about the limits of training. None of the training programs at Renaissance or elsewhere was designed to replace or rebuild that missing inner compass. Throughout 1985, I wondered how this might be done.

Part II: Generating Jobs

Chapter 6

Renaissance Goes into Business

"Hello, is this the Smith residence? My name is James Wonder and I'm the manager of the Renaissance Cleaners. We do high-quality carpet cleaning, and have over 14 years of experience in field. We currently are offering a holiday special of two rooms and a hall for only $49.95. This is not only a low price, but a good investment: maintenance of your carpets not only enhances their beauty, but extends their life—protecting your investment. So, Ms. Smith, how many rooms do you have to be cleaned before the holidays?"

It was December 1982, and Jay, Don, and I were gathered in the Renaissance offices with James Wonder and Raymond Falving, the managers of the Renaissance Cleaners, our first business venture. James and Romeo were trying out a telemarketing campaign to bring new orders for carpet cleaning. Romeo suggested that we join in the telephoning and offered a 10% commission for each new order. "Can't I get my carpet cleaned instead?" Don joked.

We all were enthusiastic about the Cleaners. To hell with relying on private grants or government grants. We would generate our own revenues to operate Renaissance. We also would generate new jobs.

Our interest in new job generation through new businesses was rooted partly in data on job creation recently released by a research team at the Massachusetts Institute of Technology. This team, headed by Professor David Birch, found that in urban economies throughout the United States, the main job generators were not established firms, but new business start-ups. Small firms, defined as firms with fewer than 20 employees, were responsible for more than 65% of new jobs. New firms, defined as firms less than four years old, were responsible for more than 75% of new jobs. For Renaissance we envisioned a series of businesses that would generate jobs directly and serve as models for other community groups. The jobs in fact would be targeted at the harder-to-reach inner city unemployed. They would serve primarily as way stations, enabling the unemployed to build work records and work habits and move into other, unsubsidized employment.

Between 1982 and 1984 we launched five business ventures. They ranged from carpet cleaning to cable manufacturing to messenger service, business machine repair service, and a convenience store.

The Renaissance Cleaners was our first venture.

One Saturday afternoon in December 1981, while I still was working downtown, a crew of young men in their early twenties came to clean the firm's carpets. This is a business that Renaissance can enter, I thought. There is no expensive equipment required. The needed skills can be mastered in a short time. Most of all, the demand will be expanding with the addition of downtown office space, and Renaissance has strong contacts with downtown firms.

In the spring of 1982 Jay and I completed a business plan for the Cleaners. It documented the increasing demand for commercial and residential cleaning in the San Francisco area. It surveyed the competition and pricing structure and set out marketing strategies. The plan was completed in May and submitted to the San Francisco Foundation. In September the foundation approved a grant of $20,000 to Renaissance as seed capital. We were on our way. Shortly thereafter, we received an additional $10,000 grant from the Columbia Foundation.

Our first step was to hire a general manager. We wanted someone with limited financial resources, who might not otherwise be able to start a business on his or her own. At the same time, we knew that this person needed experience in carpet cleaning and ambition to direct a business.

We ran an advertisement in the *San Francisco Chronicle* and received over 30 responses. The time was now October 1982, unemployment was climbing to over 8% locally (and 10% across the nation), and at least half of the applicants had college diplomas, some with master's degrees.

We decided on two who had limited education, little money, but strong presence and ambition. James Wonder, 33, had hit hard times when he came to Renaissance. He was living on welfare, eating at the downtown missions, living in a cheap downtown hotel. Yet, he talked knowledgeably about carpet cleaning and had good experience. He had worked for 8 years as chief of the janitorial crew at the University of Santa Clara. He then returned to New York to start his own janitorial service. The service fell behind in its payment of federal and state taxes and was closed down. We thought that with Renaissance backing, this business mistake could be avoided.

Ray Falving, 34, was an immigrant from Romania, who had been in the United States for five years. He had done odd jobs in carpet cleaning and janitorial work, and had operated a carpet cleaning business out of his garage. Like James, he seemed to have the drive to succeed. He was to focus on marketing, with James focusing on operations.

They came on payroll in November, each with a base salary of $1,500. We purchased a van for $3,200 and leased carpet cleaning equipment for $265 per month. We started soliciting customers.

The market proved more difficult to penetrate than we had envisioned. We had not done a thorough job in studying the cleaning contracts in downtown buildings. Most of the carpet cleaning and janitorial work in these buildings was done not through individual firms but through building managers. In turn, most of the building managers were tied into long-term contracts with the city's large cleaning and janitorial companies, particularly American Building Maintenance and Lewis and Taylor. One of our Renaissance supporters knew the vice president of American Building Maintenance, who promised to subcontract with us for smaller jobs. But the subcontracting never materialized. American Building Maintenance had no reason to help Renaissance.

Through the first months of 1983, job orders came in for cleaning, but they lagged behind projections and behind costs. We billed $1,900 in January, $2,300 in February, and $4,000 in April. Our costs were running at $6,500 per month. The telemarketing campaign produced a few orders, but they were mainly one-time orders that did not bring a regular monthly income. By the end of April, we had exhausted our capitalization. We laid off the marketing manager, Raymond Falving.

The operations manager, James Wonder, performed the tasks of both sales and operations, and the business carried on. Sales dropped to $2,000-3,000 per month, but so did costs. For a number of months, Wonder took only $750-$1,000 in salary and did much of the cleaning work himself.

The quality of the cleaning work was high: we often received compliments. "I'm going to recommend the Renaissance Cleaners to all the other motels," the owner of the Travel Lodge called to say. Yet, our quantity of work lagged. After our approaches to the downtown high-rises were unsuccessful, we turned to the neighborhood businesses: banks, retail stores, offices. Among these we thought we would have a strong marketing edge because of our social goals. We thought that potential customers would be attracted to our self-help approach. But this rarely proved to be the case. Potential customers complimented Renaissance on our goals but only infrequently purchased our service.

We tried breaking into janitorial work and bidding on janitorial contracts for the public housing units. We pointed out that many of our Cleaners lived in these units. But contracts are awarded entirely on the basis of low bid, and we were not the lowest bid. We thought that nobody could have lower costs than we had. But the janitorial market is highly competitive. The barriers to entry are low, and overhead is small throughout the industry. The nonunion firms mainly pay the minimum wage.

As our work load fell behind projections, I became more involved in the marketing and sales. I called developers and lawyers representing developers hoping that they might take an interest in Renaissance and give us even a part of their downtown buildings. I wrote to the Apartment House Owners Association, and the Office Building Managers Association. I mentioned the Cleaners in every conservation I could. "You had to graduate from Oxford to sell janitorial services?" my friend attorney Dan Martinez, kidded. "It's creating more jobs than anything you lawyers are doing," I replied laughingly. Unfortunately, though, my sales efforts were not pulling us out of the red.

Further, our efforts to reach the harder-to-employ inner city young people also were running up against needed business efficiency. To be sure, we never had a dearth of applicants for the five cleaning positions available. When we started the Cleaners, some persons thought that we would have difficulty finding minority young people willing to do janitorial work ("slave jobs" for $4.00-$5.00 an hour). Yet, we always had a list of applicants who wanted to work in the janitorial field.

But poor work habits were not easily changed, as in the case of Patrick Martin. One of the first persons to come through Renaissance's doors in 1982, Patrick was sent to four job openings, without success. Not only was there his disheveled appearance and inability to read; but also, he couldn't be anywhere on time. With the Cleaners, though, we thought that he could work under our close supervision and gradually assume responsibility.

James Wonder was hesitant to hire him ("Mike, why are you sending me these losers? I've got a business to run") but agreed. Patrick was as enthusiastic as he ever gets ("That sounds nice to me"). Within days, James was complaining about Patrick's absences and tardiness. I called Patrick, who said he was sick one day and couldn't find his shoes on the other. We might have brought Patrick along gradually; but there was carpet cleaning and janitorial work to be done: our customers didn't want to hear of Patrick's problems. Patrick was let go.

Despite these disappointments, the Cleaners received new life in September, through the federal Emergency Jobs Act. The act was designed to provide immediate employment for the unemployed. Renaissance Cleaners received $40,000 to create immediately five new positions in operation and sales and to purchase another cleaning unit.

In the next three months sales did climb steadily to over $4,600 in November and $4,000 in December. Paul Rosenblum, formerly the administrative assistant to Governor Jerry Brown, came to the Cleaners and was so taken by its aims that he agreed to do sales for a few months. "You know I saw Governor Brown's aide working for your Cleaners," an aide to a local assemblyman told me, "It's good he's doing real work instead of politics." Paul secured contracts with three local bar/restaurants for $2,200 each month. By January 1984, the Cleaners finally was near break-even point, with a staff of ten.

At this point, though, James Wonder announced that he was leaving. He had conflicting explanations. At one time, he needed to go on to another challenge: he had "succeeded" with the Cleaners, and now he wanted to move on. At other times, he was "burned out", he had put in so much time and effort and scrambling, and now he wanted a more secure job.

We tried to talk him into staying but were unsuccessful. It became a messy split. His contract called for $1,500 per month. During 1983 there were four months when he had taken less, to keep the business alive. This was known and admired around Renaissance. Now he wanted the difference, totaling $2,500. He hired an attorney, who threatened to take us before the Labor

Commission and to sue us. We angrily told the attorney to do so. In the end, a settlement was reached.

Shortly after, James stopped by Renaissance. He said he didn't want any hard feelings, that he had been able to land a job in a large carpet cleaning firm. He promised to keep in touch. It would be four months before we saw him again.

To take James's position, we promoted the head janitor, Malcolm Mitchell, 36. Malcolm resembled James in possessing background in janitorial work, an impressive presence, and ambition to run the business. Upon his promotion, he told me how much he wanted to do something for inner city youth and how he liked Renaissance's self-help approach. He had no business background, but it was clear that he could acquire needed skills quickly.

Over the next month, though, he was absent from the business for periods of time. Always he had earnest explanations. One time he was in the hospital. Another time, the business vehicle stopped running and he spent time fixing it. A third time, he was trying to sell our first cleaning unit. Additionally, he began asking repeatedly for advances. One day he needed rent money; another day, his brother was sick; still another day, he needed money for his electricity bill.

By the second month, excuses were joined by serious business shortcomings. No payment was made for two months on the cleaning van that we leased. It was scheduled to be repossessed. Malcolm's response was to hide the van two blocks away, so that the leasing company could not find it. To save money on insurance payments, Malcolm simply put the insurance bills back into their envelopes. When the van needed repairs, he took it not to a repair shop but to a gas station (that charged double).

By March, the Cleaners was taking in $3,300 in revenues but losing $2,000 per month. Some board members thought the Cleaners should be closed. But I strongly opposed this. We had put so much time and effort into the Cleaners. We could avoid the past business mistakes and establish the needed financial discipline.

Then came the "missing deposit" in the sale of the first cleaning unit. In March, Malcolm sold this unit for $800. Paul Briones, the finance director, and I assumed that the money was deposited in the business account. But in going over the books in April, we noticed no deposit. When we questioned Malcolm, he explained that, well yes, he had made no deposit, he had kept the money, but he did have plans to use the $800 for the business in the future.

It was time to end Malcolm's management. However good he sounded, and however much we wanted him to succeed, he simply couldn't be trusted. On one level, he wanted to succeed in the business, wanted to make it work. But his inclination to run scams was almost a compulsion. He had come from a street culture, trusted nobody, and seemed driven to take advantage of any opportunity to make money. "He's been playing games so long, he can't stop," was Jay's explanation.

Still not wanting to end the Cleaners, we searched for a janitorial business that might be interested in a joint venture. We advertised in the *San Francisco Chronicle* and had several responses. To our great surprise, one was from James Wonder. He wanted to come back to the Cleaners. In fact, he was willing to work without salary for a time, until the business was back on its feet.

We considered his offer but found a better one in PDR Enterprises, a recently formed janitorial business owned by

Lupe and Phil Rodriguez. Renaissance agreed to turn over management of its monthly accounts to PDR. In return, PDR agreed to take on Renaissance employees, hire Renaissance participants in the future, and split profits with Renaissance. Further, PDR and Renaissance agreed to work together in marketing.

In the next two months the Cleaners took a sharp turn. Costs decreased sharply, both through more efficient purchasing of materials and through more efficient distribution of work hours. Phil Rodriguez not only was a more competent manager than Malcolm; he also had his own money invested in the enterprise. He regarded each bill or salary paid as coming out of his own pocket.

In the time since, Renaissance and Lupe and Phil Rodriguez have continued to work together. PDR Cleaners has had its ups and downs, but it continues to employ seven to nine persons.

During much of the time that the Cleaners was struggling in 1983 and 1984, Renaissance also was struggling with another business venture, Renaissance Cable Division. Its experiences parallel many of the Cleaners' experiences and carry some of the same lessons about businesses run by community groups.

The cable division was born in the spring of 1982. Renaissance was developing its computer technician training and approaching employers. The chief of a computer consulting firm took an interest in Renaissance, and particularly in our ideas of self-supporting businesses. He suggested a business to assemble cable connectors for computer systems.

Our research indicated it to be a promising business, both financially and for Renaissance's employment goals. In 1983, U.S. sales of microcomputers alone reached 600,000, with a projected growth rate of 20% for the next several years. New computer systems would need interface cables to connect the different parts—printers, terminals, monitors, disc drives, modems. Because of the multiplicity of possible combinations, manufacturers of computer equipment were not supplying these interfaces. A market was being created for independent suppliers, and only a handful of such suppliers had come forward by mid-1983.

The product was ideal for Renaissance's employment objectives. Cable assembly was labor intensive. It taught skills in reading schematics, soldering, and basic electronics skills that could be mastered by Renaissance's inner city population and were valuable in the wider labor market. Further, the needed capital equipment cost less than $20,000.

Again, we developed a business plan and submitted it to foundations. Months passed, and numerous presentations were made to foundation officials. In December 1982, Bank of America Foundation granted Renaissance $20,000 (and a loan of $10,000) to start operations.

We interviewed widely for the general manager position and hired Donald Glenman, a former production manager from Varian. He was not from an inner city background, but in this technical area, we did not find inner city candidates. We felt fortunate to find him, for he had high- level production experience and was enthusiastic.

Also, we were able to obtain marketing advice from two computer sales representatives. These men had years of experience and good reputations in the field. They explained convincingly why we should concentrate on building RS-232 cables. We set out to do so, moving quickly to put young people to work. We made over 100 cables.

The cables did not sell. After a month, fewer than 10 cables had been sold. The next month, sales increased to $868.83, but this was far below projections and below costs of $6,000. By the fourth month, initial capitalization was spent, and the business was draining Renaissance funds. By July, the cable division reached $6,000 per month in revenues and was more than $15,000 in debt to Renaissance.

Why was the cable division, so promising in theory, lagging behind projections? Three reasons stand out.

First, there were the marketing problems. As with the Cleaners, the marketing edge that we anticipated—the desire of businesses to support a cable assembly firm with social goals—did not materialize. Less than 20% of potential customers were influenced positively by our employment goals; and in fact at least an equal number were dissuaded by these goals: they did not regard it as a serious business. We came to eliminate references to Renaissance's goals in most presentations.

Second, there was the tension between employment goals and business goals. From the start, we hired four assemblers, as well as a secretary trainee. We did so in the expectation of sufficient work to keep them busy. But even when the work level was not sufficient, we tried to keep them on board at least half-time. They were not paid for sitting around—they were sent home if there was no work to do—but our labor costs were above what business necessity would dictate.

Third, there was inadequate board oversight of the business. In our belief in entrepreneurial development, we sought to hire a competent manager to whom we would give wide discretion. We initially failed to recognize that a manager competent in many areas can be deficient in some others. This was the case with Donald Glenman. He was very good in manufacturing in a large company setting. But an internal audit conducted in August showed mistakes in purchasing (he was buying in quantities sufficient for a multi million dollar firm like Varian), as well as poor inventory control and lost cables.

In September, Glenman returned to a large manufacturing firm, and Jay Jones moved from his deputy director position to take control of the division. He immediately reduced our materials cost and established inventory control. Also, in September the Emergency Jobs Act revived the division with an infusion of $45,000. This funding allowed the division to pay off debts to suppliers, to meet operating deficits without draining Renaissance, and to boost sales by hiring a full-time marketing manager.

Sales increased to over $10,000 in November. Contracts were obtained with Computerland stores, the Pacific Stock Exchange, and Zenith, to name a few. A steady crew was assembled: five assemblers, an inventory clerk, and an administrative assistant. By the end of the year, we were confident that Renaissance Cable would reach break-even point in the next two months.

Cable assembly was located in the same building as the main Renaissance offices, and one night in December 1983, I returned at 9:00 P.M. to find the crew hard at work on an order. Jay was in his office, working on a computer cash flow projection, and the cable assembling was being handled by the crew. What a picture. Ken Christian, 27, previously in and out of low wage warehouse jobs, was heading the assembly crew, speaking knowledgeably about differences in cable configurations and schematic designs. Janice Fontano, 28, on welfare for more than four years, was directing the shipping and receiving section. The crew, a collection of the unemployed, welfare recipients, and ex-offenders, was producing computer cables valued by the major computer stores.

I knew we were on the right track. In other settings these young people had been unreliable, sullen employees. But once treated as part of the business, given responsibility in it, and told they could succeed, they had shown new energy, reliability, and creativity. We will succeed, I knew that night.

Yet, over the first quarter of 1984, we were not succeeding sufficiently as a business venture. Sales did not increase, they declined slightly. During January, February, and March, the division lost over $7,000 per month. The Emergency Jobs Act subsidy had ended, and the division was now siphoning money from the Renaissance general fund. The entire organization was being pulled into the red and the continuation of Renaissance threatened.

A number of the Renaissance board members favored closing the cable division. "We'll just be throwing good money after bad," said Bill Evers, the Chief Executive Officer of Precision Technology and a Renaissance board member. "We've got to treat Renaissance as a business, not one more social program, and that includes closing operations that aren't profitable." Other board members, including the president, Bill Russell-Shapiro, agreed that Renaissance needed a business discipline but thought that we could reach break-even point, if we we could hold on. After discussion, the board decided to give the cable division three months more. Bill made a loan of $15,000 to the business, and Richard Thieriot, publisher of the *San Francisco Chronicle,* made a similar $15,000 loan.

I was relieved by the decision. Any business is an enormous investment of time, effort, and money, in this case both Renaissance and government money. To close it was to lose this investment. Also, to close the cable division would seriously undermine our whole strategy of business development. With the loans to the division from Bill Russell-Shapiro and Dick Thieriot, Jay was able to put money into marketing. Advertisements appeared in the national computer journals. Mailings were sent to computer stores throughout the state.

These efforts brought in new orders. Cable sales went higher than ever. Revenues reached $12,800 in June, $13,000 in July, and $13,500 in August. Renaissance Cable was coming to within $3,000 per month of breaking even.

The business growth, though, spawned a new problem. Jay and the marketing manager asked to purchase ownership of the cable division. They wanted to continue hiring Renaissance participants but were not willing to continue in a Renaissance-owned enterprise. "We want the chance to be the owners and build our own economic base," said Jay.

I was pulled in two directions. Renaissance was about encouraging persons to be owners, and risk takers, not only employees. Yet, Renaissance certainly couldn't turn the business over to them: the entire prospect of building a long-term business base for Renaissance—a base of jobs, opportunities, and income—would be lost.

We talked of a compromise agreement. They would invest $10,000 and obtain 60% of the division. Renaissance would retain 40% opportunities for placements, and a percentage of profits.

As we talked of compromise, though, the business was being uprooted by forces of the international economy. The cables that we were building were now beginning to be built at far lower cost in the Far East. A standard cable from an IBM personal computer to a printer, a main Renaissance Cable product, had been sold by Renaissance Cable for $17, below most of our competition. This same cable by late 1984 was coming in from Taiwan for $5, retailing for $10.

For the moment, the ownership of the division was put aside as Jay and I searched for a strategy to keep it afloat. During this time there appeared at Renaissance a quiet middle-aged man who introduced himself as Leon Willard. He had read about Renaissance's business approach in the *San Francisco Chronicle* and wanted to join us in developing new businesses. I said we didn't have any money to pay him, but he told me not to worry. "I think I can help Renaissance, and when I do, we can worry about money." This was precisely the attitude we needed.

We soon discovered that Leon possessed a wealth of business background, including work with anti poverty groups. His career had started conventionally enough. After serving in the army in the late 1950s, he attended college and went to work as a technician in the aerospace field in southern California. In the late 1960s, disillusioned with the hierarchy and waste he saw in the aerospace industry, he moved to a technician position with Lawrence Laboratories in Berkeley.

There he came into contact with Berkeleyites who were starting small businesses— health food stores, auto repair shops, food co- ops—as a way to generate jobs and to make employees owners, allowing them to buy into ownership and decision making. The use of businesses as antipoverty mechanisms attracted him.

"My father was a sharecropper in Arkansas when I was born," Leon explained in one unguarded moment. "He moved to California but was unable to find steady work. In fact he had a friend who would get him jobs and take part of my dad's salary as payment. I didn't think this was fair. I wanted to build business structures that wouldn't be handouts to the poor and would motivate their talents by making them part owners."

In 1976, with six others, Leon moved to Fresno to start a trucking firm. The firm grew to employ 15 persons, and from there Leon received an offer to work with an antipoverty group in Fresno that was starting a farmers' cooperative. The group had received over $150,000 in grants from the federal government to develop this co-op.

When Willard saw it, he was appalled. The business was top heavy, with administrators aplenty but few other employees. New equipment was purchased that was more expensive than needed. Most of all, there was no sense of urgency to make the business succeed. "How could there be urgency, when so much government money was put in so easily." Despite his disappointment with the enterprise (which eventually went under, with the loss of all government money), Willard still believed that developing businesses was the way for antipoverty groups, "I knew that, done correctly, this business strategy could yield new jobs that were not a handout to the poor."

Soon after Willard came to Renaissance, he proposed a strategy for restructuring the cable division into a subcontracting business. "As a subcontractor, we wouldn't need the money for developing and marketing a product (money we don't have). We'd still be labor intensive, and probably maintain as large a work force."

He did more than talk about the subcontracting. He developed a proposal and set about marketing Renaissance's experience and capability in cable assembly. Within two months he had arranged a major contract with California Microwave, a Silicon Valley firm that needed the assembly of telephone cables. The contract initially called for only $5,000 per month of assembling.

But Renaissance would have no marketing or inventory costs and could maintain a crew of four persons. The cable assembly business, if crippled, was saved.

Jay left Renaissance in early 1985 to start his own consulting firm, working with private small businesses. Leon took over the reins of the cable division and built it as a subcontracting effort. There were close calls: at one point California Microwave threatened to withdraw the contract when a batch of cables did not function. But Leon used his electronics background to identify the reason for the malfunctioning; and by August California Microwave staff were recommending Renaissance to other microwave companies. Cable revenues for 1985 exceeded $100,000 and would have gone higher if California Microwave had not halted production in the last quarter of 1985. "That's the downside of subcontracting," Leon noted "You're dependent on the business health of the contracting firm."

Leon also helped build up the three other Renaissance businesses that had been launched after the Cleaners and the cable division, in 1983 and 1984: Renaissance Business Machine Repair Service, Renaissance III Convenience Store, and Gold Mountain Courier Messenger Service.

Each of these businesses had less of a rocky development than the Cleaners and the cable division; in part because the first two were structured more as joint ventures with independent entrepreneurs, and in part because all benefited from the previous experiences. "A large part of business success is persistence, being able to hold on and build on experiences" Leon said during one difficult period for the messenger service in 1985.

Renaissance Business Machines arose out of Renaissance's business machine repair training course. The assistant instructor of the course, Macon Patterson, had wanted to start his own business for some time. Renaissance provided office space, secretarial help, and marketing assistance. Patterson agreed to hire Renaissance trainees. He took responsibility for meeting costs. There were no guaranteed salaries. If revenues fell short of projections, he took less pay.

The convenience store, Renaissance III, was a joint venture between Renaissance and Greenspan Enterprises, a private firm that had been operating convenience stores in San Francisco for 20 years. Renaissance brought into the joint venture the lease and assumed responsibility for day to day management. Greenspan provided instruction in purchasing and operations.

From the start, both Renaissance Business Machines and Renaissance III more than broken even. This has not been true of the messenger service, Gold Mountain Courier, a joint venture between Renaissance and another community group, Chinese for Affirmative Action, designed to recruit refugees on welfare and offer them employment (*Gold Mountain* is the Asian refugee term for the United States). Gold Mountain as a business has been hurt by the limited English skills of the refugees, though it has been helped by their courteous service (in contrast to the wild subculture of the other messenger services).

Gold Mountain operated in the red for nearly two years and was kept afloat only by working capital through the Refugee Targeted Assistance Fund. By fall 1985, though, its revenues had climbed to over $12,000 per month, it was less than $2,000 per month in the red, and its delivery force included three vehicles along with three mopeds and four bicycles. "We've reached the critical mass of customers and of staff," Leon said, and he was responsible for much of the growth. "I think we're going to make it."

By the end of 1985 the four Renaissance businesses were all in existence. Revenues for calendar year 1985 would exceed $300,000, and nearly 40 persons would be employed.

Yet, enthusiasm for the business strategy had muted among the Renaissance staff. "I think we ought to continue our businesses," Don told me, "but we're employing fewer than 40 persons. Perhaps we should look at other ways of creating jobs."

Leon was of a similar mind. He was building Renaissance Cable and Gold Mountain Courier but wondering aloud about a new direction for Renaissance. "When I first came to Renaissance, I thought that new small businesses were the answer. But Renaissance has had all of the advantages in developing private sector businesses, and we struggled to keep our heads above water. There must be other ways of generating productive work."

Indeed, by late 1985 I no longer could avoid acknowledging one obvious lesson of our experiences. The development of new Renaissance businesses was not likely to have large-scale impact in reducing inner city unemployment. We would continue to operate the four businesses, and we were starting a fifth, a job placement service (Renaissance Workers) in early 1986. But these businesses were not creating the hundreds, even thousands, of jobs needed and would not create these jobs for many years, if ever.

Chapter 7

Visions of Businesses throughout the Antipoverty World

In the fall of 1984 a middle aged black man with a shaved head covered by a red beret arrived at the Renaissance offices and introduced himself as the Reverend Jesse James. "Who is that man?" Don asked when he saw the Reverend James sitting erectly in the reception area "Isn't he a little old to be applying for the office machine repair course?"

I never had met the Reverend James. But I knew his name through the many articles that had appeared on him during the 1960s. Then he had been head of the largest antipoverty agency in the city, the Mission Rebels.

James had come to San Francisco in the early 1960s, after years of street crime in New York and stays in Attica prison. He was determined to start over and "stop other ghetto youth from messing up, from ruining their lives in crime." He persuaded a handful of Mission district young people to start an organization, the Mission Rebels, that would be run by them and be a positive force.

Within a year, there were hundreds of young men and women participating in anti-drug programs, trips to museums and Muir Woods, Youthquakes in Dolores Park. The federal War on Poverty brought millions of dollars to the Mission Rebels, and when Sargant Shriver visited, he enthused, "This is what the poverty program is all about." The group took the slogan "Please, we'd rather do it ourselves. All we ask is the opportunity."

James was the energy behind the Mission Rebels. But at the height of their growth, he began drinking heavily, and in 1968 he was arrested for carrying a concealed weapon. He resigned from the group in the early 1970s and moved to Chico, a small city in northern California. In 1982 he returned to San Francisco to start new youth projects. He took a job as a $4.50 an hour security guard and looked around.

"I want, you know, to start businesses that will employ youth from the projects, from the streets, from the unemployment office", Jesse explained the first day. "These kids most of all need jobs. They need to be debriefed from their jive of the projects and shown that they can function in a work setting." As well as jobs, Jesse talked of economic self-sufficiency for blacks. "Black folks in particular need to see that they can build businesses on their own and not be dependent on others." He talked of starting a large general store in an inner city area or a security guard firm.

Soon after Jesse came to Renaissance, other antipoverty leaders came with similar ideas of starting businesses to generate jobs and income. An article on the Renaissance businesses appeared in the *Harvard Business Review,* and other articles and editorials appeared in the *San Francisco Chronicle* and *San Francisco Examiner.* The antipoverty leaders came with a common message: We want to start businesses, we want to be independent of government funding, and most of all we want to create jobs. Over and over, we heard, **"Our people need jobs"**.

In the Fillmore district in 1982, a rash of street robberies by young people darting in and out of the housing projects ("the barbery pirates"), gave rise to Operation Contact, an anticrime agency. The Operation Contact director came to Renaissance with the idea of a handyman business that would do miscellaneous repairs for apartment complexes. "Many of our youth don't have a good orientation to work, or any work experience," the director said. "By working for our handyman company, they'll build a job record, to get other jobs."

Morissiana West operated a storefront school on Divisidero Street in the heart of the Fillmore. The director came to Renaissance with the idea of a recycling business. "A lot of agencies get lazy and wait for the government. I don't want to do that. I figure I can be as good a businessman as anybody else."

Other directors came representing the Recreation Center for the Mentally Handicapped, the Community Mental Health Department, and the Deaf Counseling and Advocacy Referral Agency (DCARA). The director for the mentally handicapped complained, "Many of our adult clients have nothing to do all day. The best therapy for them would be work." The Community Mental Health Department director agreed. "The city pays psychiatrists $40 an hour to treat our clients on social security insurance. The clients would be far better off if they worked even part- time." The director of DCARA, himself deaf, rattled off a number of business ventures he hoped to do, a restaurant, a bookstore, a computer repair firm, adding, "Deaf people can do anything."

How good these ambitions sounded. How good to hear people in the antipoverty world speak of generating new wealth, new jobs, not worrying only about redistribution. How much both Leon and I wanted to be of help.

But should we encourage these businesses? The Renaissance businesses, starting with many advantages of contacts and expertise, had struggled to break-even and continued to struggle to stay even. More disturbing was the experience of other antipoverty agencies that had launched businesses. A quarter or so of these agencies had succeeded in breaking even. The others, the great majority, had fallen short and closed after government subsidy ended, some losing hundreds of thousands of dollars for the agency.

The idea of business ventures by antipoverty agencies was a part of the War on Poverty programs of the sixties. Title VII of the Economic Opportunity Act of 1964 created funding for community development corporations (CDC's). The CDC's were empowered to revitalize low income areas, and one strategy was the establishment of for-profit businesses. These businesses would provide services needed in the neighborhood, as well as jobs and income.

The CDC businesses were in a variety of fields: painting companies, trucking companies, janitorial companies. They received tens of thousands, even hundreds of thousands of dollars in government subsidies. Unfortunately, like many parts of the War on Poverty, these business ventures kept little data on results. David Carlson, a high- ranking domestic advisor to President Johnson, comments, "It's amazing what little scrutiny there was of CDC's that used government money to launch businesses." From his experiences he estimates that fewer than 10% of these business ventures ever reached break-even point. "Most went through government money and then closed down." [1]

Data do exist on two large-scale business development attempts by antipoverty groups in the 1970s. The first of these was the National Supported Work Demonstration, sponsored by the Department of Labor and the Ford Foundation, from 1975 to 1981. Supported work was even more ambitious than the CDC's. It sought businesses that would employ the hardest-to-reach groups—ex-offenders, ex-addicts, long-term welfare recipients. Over 60 supported work businesses ranging from selling Christmas trees and making pottery to sophisticated machine maintenance, were established in 13 cities.

In a 1981 report, Setting up Shop, Harvey Shapiro, a social scientist, analyzed both the training and business results of these ventures. As training programs, they often did provide structured work experience, and more than one-third of the hard-core participants in supported work moved into unsubsidized jobs. As independent businesses, though, the ventures were almost uniformly failures. Most generated between 25% and 35% of costs, requiring government subsidy for the remainder. When the Reagan administration ended supported work subsidies in 1980, fewer than one-fourth of the businesses continued on their own.[2]

In 1979 the Carter administration with much fanfare operated the Youth Entrepreneurship Initiative Demonstration. Concocted by Carter's Department of Labor, it was designed to show that with federal government capitalization, inner city groups could operate successful businesses. Hundreds of thousands of dollars were pumped into a string of automotive repair shops in California, a restaurant in Philadelphia, a solar heating business in Phoenix, and a novelty boutique in New York.

By all accounts the demonstration was a spectacular failure. The auto repair shops went through the government money in less than 18 months and closed. For example, an auto repair shop established in Van Nuys, California in June 1979, closed in February 1980 after spending its $48,000 in government funds. It left debts of over $5,000. The other three businesses continued for a longer time, generating up to one-half of costs, but only the boutique continued after the government money ended.

Why such a dismal business record?

A study of the Youth Entrepreneurship Initiative Demonstration by Public/Private Ventures of Philadelphia identified some of the same business difficulties that Harvey Shapiro identified in his study of supported work. First, there was the trade-off between training goals and business goals. The businesses were concentrated in labor-intensive fields—janitorial, packaging, demolition work—in which the profit margin was small and the competition fierce. New businesses in these fields typically started with a thin management structure, a minimal number of employees, and wages at the minimum wage ($3.35 an hour). In contrast, the antipoverty agencies maintained larger payrolls, seeking to maximize job creation and entrepreneurial opportunities, and paid higher wages of $4.50 or $5.00 an hour.

Not only did most of the antipoverty agency directors possess no business experience, but also they hired managers from social service backgrounds rather than business backgrounds. Further, there was little pressure on the agencies to succeed. Flush with federal government support, they did not take the financial risks that drive other private sector businesses.[3]

Since the Reagan administration took office in 1981, there has been no antipoverty business effort in the mold of these previous ones. However, the idea has not died. Rather, it has assumed a grass-roots form, with local antipoverty agencies piecing together foundation grants as seed capital, and developing businesses on their own.

Taken as a whole, these businesses have been more successful than previous efforts. With less financial cushion, they have been under truer business pressures to break even. Aware of past antipoverty experiences, they have operated more on a market basis and less on a social welfare basis.

Some examples of successful ventures. In Cincinnati the New Life Youth Services, an inner city agency, launched a pallet manufacturing business (Freedom Factory) in 1981, and by 1984 it was generating jobs for sixteen young people, without government aid.[4] The venerable Hull House Association of Chicago has been operating a mass-mailing business (Spread the News) employing ten young men and women without subsidy since 1983. In Wisconsin, the community group Advocap operates a storm window manufacturing enterprise with 12 young employees. In San Francisco, Chinatown Resources Development Center operates a janitorial firm (Maintrain), employing 14 Indochinese immigrants in a self- sufficient venture.

Yet, though the business development today is an improvement over the past, the majority of antipoverty agency business ventures are not succeeding. They are not reaching break-even point, and their jobs are proving short-lived. In the early 1980s a coalition of Bay Area foundations invested nearly $200,000 in an electronics assembly venture (Q-tronix) by the Oakland Chinese Community Council. Within two years the business had gone through its capitalization and closed. Self- Help for the

Elderly started a janitorial business with $40,000 in govern-
ment subsidies in 1984, and it was closed within a year.

In the summer of 1984, the National Center for Neighborhood
Enterprise, a group based in Washington, D. C. brought together
community group directors from across the nation who were involved in starting or operating businesses. There were directors
from Camden, New Jersey, from Seattle, Houston, New York,
and Los Angeles. They described proudly their businesses in
brush clearance, construction, mushroom growing, and restaurant service.

The talk at the conference was different from the talk at most
gatherings of antipoverty groups. It was not of social services
and calls for more government aid; rather, it was of job generation and risk-taking and profitability. "What a change from the
social worker mentality of the past," exclaimed conference organizer Robert Woodson. "It's so good to hear inner city folks
talk of building businesses of their own that are not dependent
on the government."

Yet, behind this enthusiasm for business, lay a more sobering
reality. The great majority of the business enterprises were
employing fewer than a handful of persons and were not yet at
break-even point.

The director of the antipoverty business in Camden, New Jersey was one of the most enthusiastic supporters of businesses
by community groups. He had grown up in Camden, majored in
social work in college, and worked for a number of years in a
counseling agency for young delinquents. "I saw there was something missing in what we were giving kids," he noted at the conference. "The kids weren't being taught how they could make
money on their own. It might be snowing and a kid would come
to me and say he didn't have any money. The kid didn't recog-

nize that he had a golden opportunity to make money by shoveling snow. The social work mentality wasn't teaching this. By starting businesses the kids could earn money, develop entrepreneur skills, and make money for the agency."

His talk did sound good in its emphasis on generating new jobs. Additionally, he was convincing about the training value of his businesses: even if the young people didn't go out and start businesses, their experience in his would make them better employees elsewhere. However, when I asked for financial data on his businesses, he became vague. Later I learned that they had only four to five employees each, and only the restaurant had reached break-even point after three years. The others were losing money, and the pizza parlor was ready to close.

The director was sticking with the businesses, and through persistence he might reach break-even point. But there remained, sadly, the gap between the high ideas and rhetoric of self-sufficiency and job generation and the reality of the harshly competitive new business environment.

Leon and I talked about these experiences (and our Renaissance experiences) with the antipoverty agencies that came to us in 1984 and early 1985. "We've made nearly every mistake possible in our businesses; and seen hundreds of mistakes in other antipoverty businesses," I said, only partly in jest. "If, after hearing all this, you still want to start a business, we'll work with you," Leon added. We first offered to help with the business plans. "The first step is to understand the industry you're thinking about: the competition, the wage and price structure, the marketing approaches," Leon explained. He urged each director to come back after obtaining initial information.

Nearly a year later, only a few of the directors have pursued their ideas or started businesses. Operation Contact has not gone beyond its idea of a handyman business, nor has the Recreation Center for the Mentally Handicapped proceeded on any of its ideas. The Community Health Service held a series of planning meetings, but so far nothing has come of them.

The DCARA did launch a small bookstore and videotape shop, specializing in items for the deaf, on the site of its administrative offices. But it employs only two to three persons. Leon has been working with the director, Jack Levesque, and reports, "They are finding, as other community groups have found, that the businesses they initially talked about—janitorial, restaurant, printing—are very competitive. I think they need to look to services in which deafness is an advantage."

The Reverend Jesse James decided to focus on the security guard business. He brought together three other black men with experience in the security field, announcing, "We're going to create a minority- owned security firm that is fair to employees. We're going to treat employees as potential partners, not only as bodies." Armed with these ideals, Jesse, nonetheless has encountered difficulty in getting the venture off the ground. None of the four initial partners has come up with the $500 needed in test fees and permits needed to start the business.

Renaissance has a business loan fund, Renaissance Ventures, to which Jesse applied for a loan of $1,000. The loan committee was impressed by Jesse's ideas for self-sufficiency. But when they discovered that neither he nor his partners had invested any money, they voted to wait until this investment had been made. "We can't responsibly invest in this business if the partners don't have any money of their own at stake," the loan chair, Barbara Morrison said. Barbara had seen business ventures by community groups in the 1960s and 1970s and how they had gone through government money. "If Jesse and his partners don't have their own money invested, they won't under the same pressure to succeed; and if they can't come up with $500, they won't have a business no matter what we do."

Jesse was disappointed by the committee's decision, but within a week he was back to his usual enthusiasm and plans. He talked of raising the $500 among his partners. He talked of his ideas for marketing the business. He talked of his ideas for training employees, "because our guards will be dignitaries, not just tough-looking dudes. In the past I've done the agency route, but that can only go so far. Now I'm going into business. I've got plans."

NOTES — Visions of Businesses throughout the Anitpoverty World

1. David Carlson and his wife, Arabella Martinez, currently are at work on a Ford Foundation sponsored study of the financial data of CDCs. They previously have studied the CDCs and their contribution to developing leadership in minority communities. Arabella Martinez and David Carlson, *Developing Leadership in Minority Communities*, New York, Carnegie Corporation, 1983.

One of the few studies of CDC businesses was done by the National Center for Economic Alternatives, "Federal Assistance to Community Development Corporations: An Evaluation of Title VII of the Community Services Act of 1974," Washington, D.C., National Center for Economic Alternatives, 1981.

2. Harvey Shapiro, *Setting up Shop*, New York, Manpower Demonstration Research Corporation, 1981.

3. Public/Private Ventures, "Youth Entrepreneurship: Training Disadvantaged Youth in Self-Sufficient Small Businesses," Philadelphia, Public/Private Ventures, 1983.

On the limits of youth entrepreneurship approaches see also E. H. White & Co., "Youth Enterprises Feasibility Study," California State Employment Development Department, 1980.

4. New Life Youth Services, "Financial Statements Year Ended June 30, 1984 with Report of Certified Public Accountants," Cincinnati, New Life Youth Services, 1984.

Chapter 8

"Big Red's Deli"

"I had this great idea for a computer program that large law firms could use in calendaring cases. Then I did just what the Entrepreneurship Center suggested, I researched my competition." Joyce Burris had called Renaissance to relate one more disappointment in her quest to start a new business. "Over the past two weeks, I've been looking into computer programs for calendaring cases. What do I find? There's 24 computer programs on the market today in competition with me. If it ain't one thing, it's another."

Joyce had been a legal secretary for 16 years when she came to Renaissance in early 1985, responding to a notice about our new Entrepreneurship Center. In the first six months since graduating from the center in July, she had obtained a few contracts for computer work, proving that she could compete as a businesswoman, and "be more than a typist taking orders." Yet, she had not achieved the major breakthrough she hoped for. She thought of targeting law firms with black partners, only to conclude, "They're not large enough and they don't have any money". At one point, she called excitedly about a computer contract with a large firm, only to note a week later that "the firm reneged." "I'm going to make it," she said in December 1985, "though right now I'm barely getting by."

"We've received over 100 applications", Leon exclaimed in the third week of January 1985. Within three weeks of the announcing of the Renaissance Entrepreneurship Center, these applicants had come to Renaissance, with a wide variety of business ideas. A chauffeur came, seeking to start a limousine service. A former flight attendant came seeking to start a relocation service. A bus driver wanted to start a photography service.

The applicants were persons primarily in their thirties and forties, who worked in steady, subordinate positions and dreamed of being the boss and making money. They understood the risks of starting a business but wanted to be more than employees for their working lives.

The center was designed to seek out, train, and work with aspiring entrepreneurs, especially minority entrepreneurs and those starting businesses that would be significant job generators. If effective, this entrepreneurship would expand business ownership, giving more persons a share in the market system. It would create jobs, in fact far more jobs than could be created directly by Renaissance with our five businesses.

The center offered three forms of business assistance. First, as a group, the 20-25 members of each class would attend an intensive 14 week mini business school held at night. The school would train in the skills of new business development—developing a business plan, marketing, management, finance. Second, on an individual basis, class members would work with faculty on issues specific to each business. "Renaissance should feel confident working with other small businesspersons," joked Leon, "because we've made nearly every mistake possible in our businesses, and experience is the best teacher." Third, the center boasted Renaissance Ventures, a seed capital fund that offered start-up loans of $2,000 to center graduates.

When we first announced the Entrepreneurship Center, we wondered, Will we receive any applicants? With the rush of over 100, we found ourselves faced instead with choosing among them for the 23 positions available.

About 40 percent of the applicants lacked the expertise in their chosen field of business or lacked the financial resources to possess a realistic chance of starting a business in the near future. For example, a waiter and a gardener/gourmet cook in partnership came to Renaissance seeking to start a Cajun restaurant. What was their experience in the restaurant business? "We like to cook." By their own estimates, the restaurant would cost $40,000 for only "a hole in the wall." How much could they invest? "We don't have any money to invest, we want to get a bank loan."

Another applicant, a secretary at Golden Gate University, wanted to start an employment service, placing persons in jobs for a fee. Her experience amounted to a short stint as a volunteer job developer with a nonprofit agency serving ex-offenders. She estimated her capital needs at a hopelessly inflated "$400,000 to $500,000." Did she have this amount of money to invest? "I don't have any money to invest, I'm going to get a bank loan."

A third applicant, a janitor, listed "janitorial business" as his proposed field of business. Yet, a week later when he was interviewed, he talked of starting a beauty supply business. During the week, the applicant's friend had suggested that beauty supplies were always in demand and he could make a fortune. So the applicant, who wanted to start some business, changed his mind. How did he intend to finance his business? "I'm going to get venture capital money."

In each of these cases we urged the applicants to do additional research on competitors in their proposed business fields. They should return to us in three months, when a new Center class would start.

Meanwhile, the 23 applicants chosen—representing business ideas ranging from limousine service, to janitorial services, to commercial painting, to specialty cakes—started the center's mini business school in February, 1985. They attended class two nights a week in a wood-paneled boardroom in the Bank of America World Headquarters. The downtown setting was important. "During the day, I'm a bus driver; but at night I'm an executive," commented a participant who drove the Samtrans bus during the day but wanted to develop a photography service.

During the next four months, enthusiasm remained high and attendance averaged over 85%. Participants researched and wrote business plans, studied financing mechanisms, practiced marketing and sales strategies, discussed hiring and motivating employees. They also encouraged one another and critiqued one another's business ideas. In early June, 21 of the 23 participants completed the course; 6 had started businesses during the four months; 8 others did so by the end of 1985.

Eric Jones, the chauffeur who came to the center seeking to start a limousine service, started Chauffeur Tour Guide Services in May. During the class he abandoned his idea of buying limousines in favor of a chauffeur service that used the client's car. "As I went through the cash flow projections," Eric explained, "I found that the numbers just didn't add up. The stretch limo cost $45,000, and the formal limo cost $30,000. It was too much debt for the business. Then one night, it hit me that a less expensive way of starting was to chauffeur a person in his or her own vehicle. A visitor wouldn't have to worry about getting lost or parking, and with the big push against drunk driving, someone could drink and leave the driving to us."

Chauffeur Tour Guides started slowly, with revenues of only $700 per month for the first few months. "We advertised in the newspapers and the motor inns, but only a few persons called us," Eric reported, "During these slow periods, though, I took heart hearing of the Renaissance businesses and businesses of the guest speakers that took years to reach break-even."

Chauffeur Tour Guides did grow, reaching $3,000 per month in revenues by December 1985. Eric did the driving as well as the marketing, and his wife handled the books. Two other drivers worked for them, on call. "We're not big employers now, but I think we're on the right track," Eric said in late 1985. "I mean, you look in the phone book and see three pages of limousine services, but we're the only chauffeur tour guide service."

Big Red's Deli is by no means the only delicatessen in San Francisco, and when the proprietor, Gladys DeWitt, first came to the Entrepreneurship Center with her application, Leon and I groaned. "Another restaurant in San Francisco, just what's needed," Leon commented. The restaurant field had the highest failure rates. Gladys, though, possessed a number of characteristics unusual for center applicants. Though she worked as a clerk with the city Department of Social Services, she ran a barbecue catering service on the side. She had catered two or three major events. Further, she had $10,000 in savings to invest in the business, and a partner, a city maintenance man, who could invest $5,000. She was accepted into the center.

Six weeks into the training, though, she appeared at Renaissance to show us a lease she was preparing to sign on a retail space on Eddy Street near Jones, in the downtown Tenderloin district—the run-down central city district, home to the shabby residential hotels, adult bookstores, drug dealing, and prostitution. Should she take this space?

Consider a few factors, we warned. On the plus side, the rent was $500 per month, very low by San Francisco standards, and she could have a five-year lease. New luxury hotels, including the Ramada Renaissance Hotel, were coming into the area, bringing additional foot traffic. On the minus side, was she prepared to deal with the drug addicts and street hustlers who probably would come into the shop? Was there enough foot traffic to support the business until the new hotels were open? We suggested that she study the foot traffic in the area and talk with nearby store owners. She should go through the numbers, to measure the costs against expected revenues.

Within a week, she had signed the lease. "I went to the area and studied the foot traffic, which was constant until ten at night, and I just knew this was the right location for me," she said. She hadn't completed the cash flow projections, but she was confident that "with so many people walking around, I can't miss." I located an instructor to work with her on the cash flow projections and held my breath. Gladys had taken a leave of absence from her job at the Department of Social Services, leading Leon to joke, "Are we encouraging participants to create jobs or lose them?" None of us laughed.

Four months later, Big Red's Deli had the look of a shoe-string operation. Two rickety wood tables with chairs stood at one side of the room. An uneven wood counter was in the center, flanked by an aged freezer, with an arrangement of soda pop bottles, milk cartoons, and half a watermelon.

Yet, there was a steady stream of customers. In a half-hour Gladys greeted ten customers, knowing half by name. An article on entrepreneurs had appeared in the *San Francisco Chronicle* a few weeks before, with a picture of Gladys. Gladys and her partner both worked at the deli, and they had hired two other employees part-time.

One of the employees, James, had been referred by Renaissance. He was 19, from Hunters Point, with no prior work experience. Gladys complained that he was slow in making sandwiches, and "showed no initiative." "He does what he's told, but if I don't tell him what to do, he sits on the broom." He had met the previous day with a Renaissance job counselor, and Gladys agreed to give him another week to shape up. "I need someone energetic like me," she noted.

She had completed her business plan and expected her loan application for $30,000 to be approved. A classmate from the Entrepreneurship Center, an interior designer, had suggested that she could improve the interior inexpensively with a new coat of paint; so with her partner Elmore, she had added a bright coat of red. Already she talked of opening a second Big Red's Deli, somewhere else in the City. "People who know barbecue tell me that my ribs are the best around, better than Leon's Barbecue or Kansas City Barbecue."

Joyce Burris came to the Entrepreneurship Center with the idea of starting a bed and breakfast inn. She estimated her capital needs at over $200,000, while acknowledging that she had no money of her own to invest and no experience in the field. Though Leon and I both regarded the bed and breakfast as highly unrealistic, we were impressed by Joyce's determination to become a businesswoman. "I've got a steady job, but I want to be the one making decisions and I want to take the chance to make some real money." Leon argued in her favor as we considered admissions: "She's unlikely to do the bed and breakfast, but through the center she may find a more appropriate idea." Within a few weeks she abandoned the bed and breakfast and talked of two new ideas. One was fashion design for large women. She liked to design fashion patterns and received compliments from friends. She talked of making prototypes of her designs and marketing them to the Neiman-Marcus and Macy's stores. At the same time, she talked of forming a business that would incorporate her skills as a legal secretary.

We encouraged her to focus on one idea. Against our hopes, she chose the fashion design and set off to sell her designs. After two months and no orders, she decided she needed a business more closely tied to her legal secretary skills. She saw a need for computerizing legal offices and set off to structure a business that marketed computer programs to law firms. She expected little competition, but in her market research she soon found tens of sophisticated firms in the field. She did obtain contracts with law firms for computer work, though these contracts primarily were in word processing. By the end of 1985, she remained confident in her energy and abilities to succeed, but still searching for a place in the market.

In all, 14 of the 21 graduates of the first center class were in some business by the end of 1985, six months after graduation. The majority were struggling to reach break-even point; even with their strong motivation. For example, the bus driver came to class regularly and completed a business plan for his photography business, but he found orders few. "He's the nicest, most motivated guy in the world," said Leon, "but the quality of his photography is not high. He needs to improve this quality."

Yet, if struggling, the entrepreneurs were moving forward, generating jobs and goods. Seven of the 14 had hired other employees. The second center class was completed in December, and within three months 13 of the 22 graduates were in business.

At a year-end center gathering, five or six of the entrepreneurs noted how the center enabled them to avoid mistakes made by other novice entrepreneurs. Eric Jones avoided costly expenditures on limousines. Another participant, Hana Kawaguchi, dropped her initial idea of a retail dress shop, in favor of a mail order business. "I probably saved $80,000 that I would have lost on the shop," she later commented.

Nearly all of the entrepreneurs talked of how, otherwise isolated, they were able to draw encouragement and ideas from one another. In her mail order business, Hana Kawaguchi carried the jewelry produced by Verena Brooks (Modus Vivendi), another participant. Through his commercial painting business, Armando Zelaya (Armando's Painting) made referrals to Jose Preza's *Homeowners Montage* real estate magazine.

Armando Zelaya, Jose Preza, and the other center graduates were not drawn from the lowest income inner city populations coming to Renaissance's training programs. Yet, what of potential entrepreneurs among this population? Were there women on welfare or men on public assistance who could start and succeed in businesses, who could carve out jobs for themselves and perhaps for others?

In the first Entrepreneurship Center cycle of 1986, eight low-income, unemployed men and women enrolled. Among these participants, Ernest Love, a sometime janitor then on public assistance, came to the center with the idea of starting a janitorial company or a beauty salon. His friend Greg Richardson, a sometime longshoreman, wanted to start a limousine service. Antoinette Butler, receiving government disability insurance envisioned a retail store on Third Street in Hunters Point, while Cleo King, a retired janitor, envisioned a retail cookie shop, also in Hunters Point. Imago Wilson, an ex- offender working part-time as a chauffeur, was determined to start a limousine business.

Imago had written on his application:

"Im a self starter. I also have access to large numbers of people Through my fathers church organization...I no I would be able to get the financing which has always been a setback, but more than anything your program would provide one with the skills to speak the busines language."

Despite this enthusiasm for business training, Imago could not stay focused on limousine driving. He kept trying to link a limousine business with producing records for famous rock music stars he claimed to know. One day he called to say he was arranging a fund-raiser for Renaissance with his friend Boz Scaggs. Another day, he was close friends with the rock group Journey. He failed to do any of the written assignments and missed class sessions. Imago dropped out before the completion of training.

Five of these eight lowest-income participants completed the class, though only three were able to compile any type of business plan. Over the next six months each struggled to start an enterprise. Ernest Love called Renaissance at all hours with schemes to operate his proposed beauty salon twenty-four hours a day ("We'll be the only beauty salon open twenty-four hours") and to raise $25,000 in start-up costs from "rich San Franciscans." Greg Richardson went through a variety of business ideas—a restaurant, a transportation service for the elderly, a janitorial service—before returning to the transportation business. Near the end of training, he wrote to Mayor Feinstein and Governor Deukmejian asking for help in raising $40,000.

Yet, among these participants, some business activity developed. Cleo King, the "cookie man," started selling cookies from his house and, by the sixth month, was investigating the consignment of cookies to local stores. Antoinette Butler had abandoned her highly risky retail store idea for a more realistic partnership with an existing store. Even Greg Richardson joined as a partner in a new business offering typing and filing for offices.

Near the end of the training cycle, I asked my father-in-law, Marvin Levin, to be a guest speaker. In 1971, Marvin joined with three business associates to start Consolidated Capital, a real estate syndication firm. Consolidated Capital started with a three-office "suite" in downtown Oakland. Over the next 15 years, Consolidated Capital grew to be one of the largest real estate syndication firms in the world, employing over 600 persons in a company-owned high-rise in Emeryville. Each of the founders had become a millionaire many times over, and the company was well known to class members.

I thought that Marvin would talk about the success of Consolidated Capital. Instead, he focused on his previous entrepreneurial ventures in the ten years before he launched Consolidated Capital. He had started six businesses, and none had been a success. One of these, a home burglar alarm business, lost over a hundred thousand dollars. He explained that among millionaire entrepreneurs, few had succeeded on their first business. However, they had learned from experiences, and continued to try new enterprises. The class discussion that followed was animated: Were there still business fields not over-populated? ("My God, yes, there always will be new business opportunities"), What was the best way to learn about a business possibility? ("Work in the field, preferably starting at the bottom"); What was the best way to learn about real estate? ("Buy my new book, preferably the hardback copy").

I knew Marvin did not hold a high regard for most anti-poverty efforts. But after class he was upbeat about the Entrepreneurship Center. This was the type of program that offered hope to inner city Oakland or other inner city areas. It was not one more government giveaway. The participants were carving out their own jobs and business ownership. The businesses might be small now. But hadn't Consolidated Capital started with four previously obscure entrepreneurs? Wasn't the risk taking and drive of the participants precisely what our policies should encourage?

Chapter 9

When Government Attempts to Create Jobs

As unemployment climbed to over 10% in late 1982, there was pressure on Congress to **do something** to reduce unemployment. The result in March 1983 was the Emergency Jobs Act of 1983, allocating $4.6 billion to government units to create jobs rapidly.

The act represented the liberal approach of reducing unemployment through public service jobs. Governments were to utilize this new money to employ the unemployed in public projects, especially public works projects. To us at Renaissance, as to many persons around the nation, the jobs act seemed like the sensible thing to do. We submitted testimony to Congress urging its immediate passage to halt the wasted energies of the over 11 million Americans out of work.

During the next two years, though, the jobs act had minimal impact on unemployment. It created very few jobs relative to the number unemployed, and at a high cost per job. Far from putting people to work immediately, the act was tied down in lengthy bureaucratic processes, union regulations, and heavy capital costs.

The Emergency Jobs Act was not the first choice of the Reagan administration to reduce unemployment in 1982 and 1983. In December 1982 the president suggested that unemployment could be solved through each employer hiring one additional person. No large scale government intervention would be needed.

"Can you believe that?" was Don's reaction as we read the newspaper reports, "Employers who are struggling to compete aren't going to take on voluntarily additional employee costs. I have a hard enough time persuading employers to hire our people when they do have jobs open."

My reaction was different. A part of Reagan's idea might be feasible. Larger businesses, businesses with over 100 employees, might have some flexibility. What if they each were to create one part-time job above their current work force. The cost per job at $4.00 per hour and 20 hours per week would be around $100 per week, including benefits, less than the weekly liquor bill for the law firms at which I had worked. At Renaissance, with only 12 employees at the time, we certainly had enough work for helping the two secretaries to keep someone busy half-time. Firms with over 100 employees should have no difficulty in avoiding make-work.

During the next month, Renaissance launched the Jobs for Youth Network. It was headed by Dick Blum, an investment banker and husband of Mayor Dianne Feinstein, and enlisted the support of the city's business and labor leaders. It urged each employer to create one part-time job. The jobs would be targeted at low income youth who were willing to go through education or job training programs in the time they were not working. A well-attended press conference was held, after which The *San Francisco Chronicle* ran an editorial in support of the Network, which stated:

> When President Reagan suggested that major cuts could be made in unemployment if every business hired just one more employee, the idea was met mostly with skepticism. Now a San Francisco ad hoc coalition has taken up the idea with the goal of making a number of unemployed young people self-sufficient . . . We urge employers who can create some part-time work to contact the program at 861-JOBS.

Following the *Chronicle* editorial, each of the seven business and labor leaders heading the network was asked to contact six employers. Only one did so. The others turned out to be too busy with their own activities and, after the press conference, did not return phone calls. It soon became clear to me that reliance on private sector volunteerism was not going to get us very far. The executives each had a business to build, and any time spent on Renaissance was dead time, it didn't generate a new client or carry out work for a client.

Our ability to generate jobs was blocked further by the complex decision making in most of the law firms we approached. We concentrated on the city's corporate law firms, because of our contacts among the senior partners and the healthy income of these firms. However, no single partner could make decisions on hiring; instead, the large law firms maintained various hiring committees. When we called on our request, it always seemed to be in committee.

After four months, we generated only twenty-six jobs, a far cry from the hundreds of jobs citywide we had expected. As for the Reagan administration, it seemed to lose interest in the volunteerism suggestion immediately after it was put forward. There was no follow-up or means of counting the jobs created.

As our Jobs for Youth Network faded by May 1983, the Emergency Jobs Act came into operation. As I talked to other inner city organizations across the nation, there was excitement that the jobs act would thin the lines of unemployed we all were seeing.

It wasn't long, though, before disturbing reports came in about the act's implementation. An initial report by the *New York Times* in July 1983 indicated that few unemployed persons were being put to work. Headed "3 Month Old Emergency Act Has Created Few Jobs," the report noted that three-quarters of the money was directed toward public works jobs, which required time in selecting, planning, and proposing projects. According to a Massachusetts state official, "If a town wants to build a library with jobs bill funds it has to hire an architect, draw up plans, hold town meetings, reach a consensus, and then submit proposals. If we talked a year from now, I wouldn't be surprised if the money was still trickling in." The *Times* commented that, although the money was intended primarily to help men and women whose jobs had been in declining industries, the early beneficiaries of the funds were lawyers, accountants, engineers, and consultants brought in to draw up proposals, plan projects, and conduct public hearings.[1]

The *Washington Monthly* similarly found delays in hiring, as well as a high cost per job, when it studied the Emergency Jobs Act in late 1983 ("Is the Jobs Bill Creating Jobs?"), nine months after the bill's passage. Jobs Act funds were divided among 60 different federal agencies. They were subject to the requirements of public hearings, land use compliance determinations, and audits, as were to the regular agency projects.

The *Washington Monthly* writer, Patricia Cohen, traced the spending of $17 million allocated to the city of Baltimore, and particularly the city's allocation of $1.2 million to renovate a publicly owned building for use by a biomedical company. A public hearing was held in mid June, and in July a plan was submitted to the federal Economic Development Administration. An environmental assessment was needed and took until late September. Bids from local contractors were solicited and did not go out until November. Cohen estimated that hiring would not begin until January 1984, at the earliest, ten months after the act's passage.

Cohen identified other shortcomings of the Emergency Jobs Act beyond delay. One was the distribution of funds with no consideration of unemployment rates, so that low-unemployment states such as North Dakota and South Dakota received higher per capita funds than the high-unemployment states of Michigan and West Virginia. This distribution reflected congressional politics that brought major grants to the districts of Appropriations Committee members. Further, the cost per job of public works projects was averaging over $40,000 per year in most cases. A $5.6 million highway project in Mississippi employed 83 people, and other water projects cost as much as $100,000 for every job created.[2]

The most extensive study of the Emergency Jobs Act has been undertaken by the U.S. General Accounting Office (GAO), empowered by Congress to monitor the Act. In early 1985 the GAO released its first of six in- depth studies of the Act's implementation, a study of the job creation in northeast Texas. The conclusions reached by the GAO echoed those of the New York Times and Washington Monthly: the job creation was slow, it was costly, and it was not highly targeted at the low income unemployed.[3]

When the jobs bill was enacted in March 1983, the unemployment in the seven-county area of northeast Texas was 14.7% or 12,344 persons. The area was awarded $3.4 million for 23 projects, primarily public works projects, such as renovating community parks and road, street and drainage improvement, weatherizing the homes of the elderly, or a new library.

These public works projects brought clearer public benefits than the largely clerical and maintenance jobs of CETA public service employment (PSE). However, the job creation was limited. By March 1984, a year after the bill's enactment , $830,000 or 25% of the money had been spent. Only 150 persons had been employed, for an average of 5 weeks. Over 90% of the participants were unemployed prior to hiring, but they were not clearly the long-term unemployed.

In late 1986 the GAO issued a final report on the act's influence across the nation. The GAO estimated that as of March 1984, one year after the bill was passed, 34,000 jobs could be attributed to the act's funds spent by that time. The employment increase attributable to the act peaked at about 35,000 jobs in June 1984, when nearly 8 million persons were employed. These additional jobs represented less than 1 percent of 5.8 million jobs created by the economy from the time the bill was passed until June 1984.[4]

One person who anticipated the inefficiencies of public works projects for immediate job creation was Alice Rivlin, an economist and the head of the Congressional Budget Office in 1983. In her testimony during hearings on the Emergency Jobs Bill, Ms. Rivlin looked at job generation under an earlier public works program, the Local Public Works program. Local Public Works contributed $6 billion to states and localities during the late 1970s to fund over 10,000 projects, principally in areas of high unemployment. The Department of Commerce estimated that Local Public Works generated 93,000 person-years of on-site project employment, plus 66,000 person-years of employment in supplying industries such as concrete and steel. Even counting the indirect employment, the cost per job was $38,000. Rivlin noted that this was consistent with the estimates by the Bureau of Labor Statistics that the average federal expenditure per job created through public works spending ranged from $39,000-$51,000 per job.[5]

As the national economy improved in 1984 and 1985, and unemployment fell to below 7.4% during much of 1985, the Emergency Jobs Act largely was forgotten. No additional funds were allocated after the first allocation in 1983. At Renaissance, we had great difficulty finding any data locally or nationally on such key questions as cost per job or evaluation of services performed. Aside from the early *New York Times* and *Washington Monthly* pieces, the Act was ignored by the press.

Yet, the act's experiences are very important as the third of three major experiences—along with the Neighborhood Youth Corps of the 1960s and the PSE of the 1970s—of public sector job creation during the past two decades. The Neighborhood Youth Corps was established in the first War on Poverty legislation of the mid-1960s and provided jobs in the public sector. These jobs were mainly in cleaning parks and beaches, assisting clerical staff, and assisting the existing government work force. Within a short time, the jobs were assailed as make-work, a charge borne out by subsequent studies. These studies found that the quality of work effort differed among work sites, but that in a significant number of work sites the young people were not supervised and sometimes not even required to work the full number of hours.[6]

The Neighborhood Youth Corps continued in reduced size until 1973 and the passage of CETA. CETA brought a more major direct job creation program, PSE, which created jobs in the public sector targeted at unemployed adults. At its height in 1979, it enrolled 1,250,700 persons in public sector jobs—752,000 at any one time—at a cost of $5.1 billion.

Proponents of public sector job creation have portrayed the participants in PSE as performing valuable tasks for their cities and gaining skills to move into other jobs. In fact nearly all of the jobs were in the services, and their value was not easily gauged. Many PSE participants did work alongside other city employees as street sweepers, as public recreation aides, and, most of all, as clerks. For the most part they functioned as other employees, and there certainly was not the loose supervision and fabricated time cards of the Neighborhood Youth Corps.[7] But neither was there clear addition to the cities' wealth. In the clerk jobs, for example, an additional hire might mean additional tasks completed. But the hire also might split existing work or save the city from hiring another employee. In a leading study of the "displacement" effect of PSE job creation, Professor Richard Nathan of Princeton University estimated that 20% of the PSE jobs were not new hires but jobs that would have been created otherwise by cities.[8]

The design of the Emergency Jobs Act was a reaction to PSE and the Neighborhood Youth Corps. By emphasizing public works, the act attempted to ensure clear addition to wealth, not a distribution of existing work. By emphasizing a lengthy planning process, it attempted to prevent the loose supervision and make-work of the Neighborhood Youth Corps. Yet, the design of the act also carried important trade-offs in the small number of jobs created and the lengthy time needed for job creation.

The Emergency Jobs Act has been the major job creation effort in the 1980's; but not the only one. On the local level, a Conservation Corps approach is being tried throughout the nation.
Bob Burkhardt, the executive director of the San Francisco
Conservation Corps, talked enthusiastically in December 1985
about his Corps:

We were landscaping the housing project in Chinatown, the Ping Yuen
project, when an elderly Chinese woman approached and handed our
corps members a box of incense in appreciation of their work. She clearly didn't have a lot of money, but she wanted to show her appreciation.
Other adults give flowers and other gifts to corps members when they
see our work. These adults worry that youth today have become lazy
or think the world owes them a living. Then they see our members,
and they think "Something is going right in this country."

It was 8:15 A.M. and we were standing outside the corps headquarters in the Golden Gate National Park. The corps is situated
on some of the most beautiful urban parkland in the world, overlooking the Bay, with a view of the fog-shrouded Golden Gate
Bridge.

For the past forty-five minutes, Burkhardt had led exercises
in a nearby playing field for the 86 corps members, all but 4 or
5 whom had assembled by 7:30 A.M. The corps members were
18-22 years old, two-thirds men and one-third women, a near
equal mix of the city's black, white, Latino, and Asian ethnic
groups (the liberal's dream outfit), all wearing the standard
corps blue shirt with a corps patch. A series of push-ups was followed by leg raises, stretching, and a one-mile run to the Marina
Green. Following these exercises, the corps members piled into
seven mini vans with "San Francisco Conservation Corps"

prominently displayed on the side. They drove to the work sites where they would work until three o'clock in the afternoon.

The corps is a form of government job creation sharply different from the Emergency Jobs Act, PSE, and the Neighborhood Youth Corps. It was formed in 1982 by Burkhardt and a group of prominent San Franciscans seeking to link job training with new job creation. Unemployed young San Franciscans were to be put to work in productive conservation and construction work, where they would develop work skills and move into other jobs.

The touchstone of the corps is discipline and structure. "Many of these kids come from households in which there is little structure, little requirement to be somewhere on time. If they are to hold jobs, they need most of all to learn work discipline," Burkhardt explains. Applicants to the corps are told to come for the daily 7:30 A.M. exercises, and if they are five minutes late, they are told to come back another time. Members who come late, even five minutes late, are given warnings, and if they are late again, they are dismissed from the corps.

When I arrive one day at 7:20 A.M., the majority of corps members already are present. Lonnie King, 19, is standing alone, looking slightly disheveled, but is talkative as exercises are about to begin. He explains that he is part of crew 6, which does landscaping work in the Glen Park area ("pulling weeds, taking care of the grass, planting"). He adds that he is planning to start his own garden someday ("You know, some vegetables, some flowers"), even though San Francisco doesn't have very good soil.

Later, Burkhardt tells me that Lonnie King is one of the people for whom the corps is made:

You could probably tell that he is mentally slow, and he hasn't had much success in anything before. But he's a nice guy, not mean at all, and he usually can work if pointed in the right direction. He was fired from the corps about six months ago for coming late repeatedly, but he did the required 40 hours of community service and came back as a "Second Chancer". Yesterday he called me at 6:45 to say "Bob, do you think I can still come in today." It was his way of saying he was going to be late. Today, though, he was here by 7:00 A.M.

Burkhardt described the disciplined structure of the San Francisco Conservation Corps as the result of his ten years in the field. Graduating from college in 1961, Burkhardt had been a schoolteacher and started an alternative grade school. In 1976, he left education to become a counselor with the California Conservation Corps (CCC). The CCC was then a new program modeled by California governor Jerry Brown after the Corps programs of the Depression. The CCC took young men and women outside of their urban neighborhoods to residential centers in rural areas for conservation work.

Over the years, Burkhardt came to envision a conservation corps that could do work in the cities and not require the high costs of a residential setting. In contrast to other government job creation, especially the Neighborhood Youth Corps, it would emphasize discipline, not be afraid to expel students, include incentives to better performance, and be sensitive to work output. Each crew would include 10-12 youth working together, headed by a crew chief with the duty of ensuring that the crew was busy.

As I talked with Bob, we were joined by John Oubre, the assistant director, who also was a former schoolteacher. Oubre talked of other young people who had been in and out of jobs, and who had acquired a discipline through the corps. "It's great for me to see youth who have failed in school start to achieve in the corps." John launched into a story about a young man who recently joined the corps. He had been in and out of trouble, and his time in the corps had been marked by a few absences. He had been counseled by staff and had come the day before by 7:00 A.M. and immediately volunteered to do any tasks, such as taking out the trash. "These kids need victories; they need positive attention. Just knowing that someone cares about whether they do a good job can mean a lot."

John continued with another story, about Derek Perry. Perry had come late his first day in the corps and had been sent home. He became abusive, yelling in front of other corps members that John was picking on him and had a bad attitude, but John only said, "There's the door, you'd better get out through it." Two weeks later, Perry came back and applied to the corps under a different name. When he was told to report the next day at 7:30 A.M. for an interview, he again began to yell that the corps was jive, until another counselor recognized him. The counselor spent time explaining that if he wanted a job, he couldn't demand attention and expect to get his way, but Perry stormed out.

As John recounted the story, I expected to hear of a successful ending. But there was no successful ending. Perry never came back, and John concluded, "He's hopefully going to grow up sometime, but I don't know what it will take."

Indeed, the discipline of the corps does not result in good work habits for everyone. One-third of the members drop out within a month of enrollment. Faced with strict rules, they do not improve work behavior.

"It's not terrible that they leave," Burkhardt believes. "Some of them have never had someone say no to them. They have to learn that poor work habits have consequences." Burkhardt describes the corps as practicing a necessary triage. "Much as I might like, we can't help everyone, and if we tried to and lowered our standards, nobody would be helped."

Burkhardt is aware that the corps serves relatively small numbers, 80-90 at any time. Is there enough productive work for a larger number? "No question," Burkhardt answers. "We have more than enough requests for the next three months from the Park and Rec. Department, from community groups that need repairs, from the National Park Service." He thinks that the corps can increase to 500 members, at four centers, if there were funding.

Funding, though is a tricky issue. In 1985, the corps received over $1 million in city funds, far more money than other community groups, which saw their funding cut. The corps has talked of ways of generating its own funds so as not to be dependent on the city. It has talked with Renaissance about developing businesses. But through 1986 no income-generating business had been created.

Though Burkhardt has ideas about extending services to senior citizens, he sees the future primarily as improving current services. "My past ten years has been spent on corps work, and I intend to spend the next ten with the corps. I like trying new things—some work, some don't—and that's how we improve the services. There always will be an age cohort, 18-23, that needs our services. I never worry about not having enough applicants looking for jobs."

NOTES — When Government Attempts to Create Jobs

1. Iver Peterson, "3 Month Old Emergency Act Has Created Few Jobs As Yet," *New York Times*, July 5, 1983.

2. Patricia Cohen, "Is the Jobs Bill Creating Jobs?" *Washington Monthly*, December 1983.

3. U.S. General Accounting Office, "Projects Funded in Northeast Texas by the Emergency Jobs Appropriations Act of 1983," Washington, D.C. General Accounting Office, 1985.

4. U.S. General Accounting Office, "Emergency Jobs Act of 1983," Washington, D.C., General Accounting Office, 1986.

5. U.S. Senate, Subcommittee on Employment and Productivity, "Hearings on the Employment Opportunities Act of 1983, " Washington, D.C., Government Printing Office, 1983.

6. Regis Walther and M. Magnesson, "A Study of the Effectiveness of Selected Out of School Neighborhood Youth Corps Programs," Washington, D.C., George Washington University, 1971. Walther and Magnesson focused on the corps program in four cities (Cincinnati, Durham, St. Louis, and Pittsburgh). They found 18% of the women and 33% of the men dropping out within the first three months. The tediousness of the jobs, the low pay, the absence of advancement opportunities were all cited as factors for dropouts.

Also, Robert Schrank *Ten Thousand Working Days*, Cambridge, Mass. MIT Press, 1978. Schrank was director of the Neighborhood Youth Corps in New York City during the mid sixties. The corps had put together a small building maintenance training program with private hospitals and sought to replicate it with city hospitals. Schrank relates: "At a meeting of the city-wide coordinating council, I reported how well this maintenance training program was working and suggested we do it at eight of the city's nineteen hospitals. It was agreed our next trial run would be at Bellevue Hospital, the city's largest. It was a total disaster because the skilled help at Bellevue mostly told our black and Puerto Rican helpers to get lost, come back at quitting time, go to the movies and so forth."

7. Michael Wiseman, "CETA Subsidized Public Employment in San Francisco," University of California, Berkeley, Department of Economics, 1979.

8. Richard Nathan, *Monitoring the Public Service Employment Program*, Washington, D.C., Brookings Institution, 1979. A leading overview of PSE is contained in Robert Cook and Charles Adams,

Public Service Employment: The Experience of a Decade, Kalamazoo, Mich. W. E. Upjohn Institute, 1985.

Part III: Urban Possibilities

Chapter 10

Me and Joe Califano: January 1985

In the fall of 1984 I decided to leave Renaissance to take a position on the staff of Congressman Howard Berman. I was fed up with the constant scramble for funds that working for a community group had become, and I had come to doubt that the local level really was the place to be.

Bill Spring had advised, "Go work on the local level." But as I watched the presidential campaign of 1984, the excitement seemed to be on the national level. If I was serious about employment policy, that was where I should be, helping to shape employment initiatives influencing millions (not hundreds) of persons. "I never could understand why you were spending time on the small scale that Renaissance involved," commented a former Harvard classmate now serving as a Department of Labor official. "Nobody's heard of Renaissance. If you want to be a player, it's time to come to Washington."

I went to see Anthony Kline, a judge on the California Court of Appeals, who had been legal advisor to Governor Jerry Brown and who knew many of the state's politicians. He wrote to Congressman Berman, and a week later I received a call from Berman. "I'm looking to take a leadership role on domestic issues," Berman announced. On Christmas Day 1984 we met in Los Angeles, and two days later he offered me a job as a legislative aide. As I could not leave Renaissance immediately, we agreed that, beginning in January 1985, I would work two weeks a month in Washington and then join his staff full-time in April.

I arrived in Washington on Sunday, January 13, 1985, when the temperature was below zero and most of Washington immobilized in a heavy snowfall. Anxious to start, I found a cab to Capitol Hill and the Longworth Office Building, and Carol Stern, Berman's administrative assistant, showed me through the staff offices.

My desk overlooked a small park, a far cry from the housing project that Renaissance offices overlooked. The offices down the hall carried the names of members of Congress regularly in the news. Now I was at the center of activity. Why had I waited so long?

That night I outlined ideas for a Berman Youth Employment Bill that would be different both from the Great Society programs of the 1960s and the inactivity of the past few years. "You can't wait to get started," Carol noted, and she was right.

The next morning I set out to meet with staff of the House Education and Labor Committee, the House committee overseeing employment issues. Bill Spring had given me the name of one staff counsel (appointed by the Democratic committee chair) who had been a congressional staffer and union official concerned with employment for 15 years. The man was friendly, and he agreed to meet me that afternoon.

"A main battle in Congress will be over the cuts proposed by Reagan in job training funds," the staffer explained. The Reagan administration had proposed funding cuts in the main job training program, the Job Training Partnership Act (JTPA). Among these cuts was the elimination of the Job Corps, a youth residential training program, and reduction of training funds for displaced workers. The House Democratic leadership opposed these cuts, and much of the staff effort would be to maintain the status quo. "We'll be fighting a rearguard action for most of 1985, trying to prevent further cuts," he said. Most of the staff time in 1984 had been devoted to similar rearguard action.

The staff, following the committee chair Congressman Augustus Hawkins, had put forward a new initiative in 1984, the Youth Incentive Employment Bill, to provide government-funded jobs for low-income youth who pursued education or job training. The jobs would be part-time during the school year and full-time during the summer. The bill's sponsors saw these jobs as encouraging low-income unemployed young people to gain immediate employment and develop skills for longer-term success.

The bill passed the House but was opposed by the Reagan administration and died. The staff was preparing to reintroduce it in 1985 but had almost no hope of its passage. Why do this? "What else are you going to do?" the staffer asked.

Later in the day I met with a woman on the staff of the Senate Labor and Human Resources Committee. She had worked for the Library of Congress research staff for several years before the Republicans took control of the Senate, and she had moved to a staff position. She agreed that the Democratic initiatives in the House were going through the motions because the administration saw them as more War on Poverty-type programs.

The administration saw inner city unemployment as best reduced through the healthy private economy and through reducing the minimum wage. The latter proposal was going to be the main employment initiative in the Senate.

"The reduction of the minimum wage," I thought. "That's not going to create new jobs in cities." Even at the current minimum wage of $3.35 an hour, most young people would not take minimum wage jobs. Working 40 hours a week, the $3.35 an hour amounted to less than $8,000 a year.

In the evening I began to doubt whether this Washington move was a good decision. Did I want to spend my time pushing employment initiatives just for the sake of doing something, when these initiatives would be vetoed by the president? Did I want to spend my time trying to convince other congressional staff that the subminimum wage was a crazy idea?

The next morning I met with another staff person on the House Education and Labor Committee. He outlined the hearings that the committee was planning to hold, especially one on the causes of youth unemployment. The hearing would bring together persons from community groups, labor unions, and businesses to testify on causes of unemployment and models for successful training. Testimony on inner city illiteracy would be a key matter. The committee would travel to locations throughout the United States.

I couldn't believe this. While waiting to talk with this staffer, I browsed through the thick books of committee hearings in 1983 and 1984. The hearings were filled with testimony on past employment programs. What more could additional hearings reveal, I thought. It might be exciting to bring together persons from throughout the United States, or travel around the country. But would testimony be more than preaching to the converted. Was this what I wanted to do with my life? Later in the day I met with a legislative aide to Representative Charles Schumer, who was sponsoring the National Entrepreneurship Bill. The bill was designed to promote new sources of financing for new businesses. According to the aide, capital markets were not working efficiently to finance new businesses. Many entrepreneurs with business ideas that could generate hundreds of thousands of new jobs could not obtain financing.

The efficiency of capital markets certainly is in need of question. The venture capital firms that receive so much publicity provide financing to only a tiny number of firms. As we had seen at Renaissance, other financial institutions are very reluctant to finance new businesses because of the volatility of the new business world. Yet, I felt uneasy listening to the aide. He had introduced himself as someone with a background in academia and as a congressional aide. He never had operated a business. He was likely to be perceived by more conservative legislators and by the Reagan administration as one more theoretical liberal with no experience in operating a business.

By the time I was to leave on Thursday evening, Washington no longer seemed the place to be for reducing unemployment. Congressman Berman had proved to be the one pleasant surprise. He was willing to question the liberal attachment to the current welfare and employment systems. But I doubted that any new initiatives were going to become law with the Reagan administration, and I didn't want to be in hearings or write memos only to go through the motions. Also, I didn't want to be like Schumer's aide or other staffers I saw: energetic, sincere, but not very convincing since their talk was mainly theory, not tied to experience.

On the plane back to San Francisco, I read *Governing America*, Joseph Califano's description of his years as secretary of health, education and welfare in the Carter administration. When I was in Washington in 1978, Califano was one of the policymakers whom the young lawyers I knew strove to emulate. Califano was a Washington insider who, during the early 1970s, developed a lucrative law practice (income over $200,000 a year) based on his connections. When Carter was elected, he stepped into a cabinet position, overseeing the key urban issues of health care, and education, as well as employment.

In *Governing America*, Califano sees himself as a humanitarian, sacrificing to help "the vulnerable Americans." Yet, his sacrifice amounts to taking a job paying more than what 90% of Americans earn, and includes a private car and private chef. When he is fired by Carter in 1979, he does not go to work on a health program or a school but returns to his Washington law practice.

More disturbing, Califano approaches all issues on a highly theoretical level. His book is a compilation of chapters on health care, abortion, civil rights, and welfare. The welfare chapter, for example, shows no understanding of how welfare operates on a local level: the dependency, the child care difficulties, the lack of skills and motivation. Anyone who has worked on the local level knows that the main problem with welfare is not the size of its payments (which are pitifully small), but its lack of expectations. Welfare officials constantly provide excuses why welfare recipients cannot work; and an inertia and lack of discipline settles into many welfare households. Any serious welfare reform would start with a work requirement. From his heights in Washington, though, Califano sees welfare as an administrative problem. He wants to consolidate the administration of different assistance programs (AFDC, SSI, food stamps) and provide fiscal relief to states. The result would be to improve the lot of welfare recipients by providing them with more money.

President Carter is portrayed by Califano as the villain of the book and as unsophisticated in welfare matters. But it is Carter who shows far greater understanding about welfare dependency than Califano. Carter immediately focuses on the job nexus. Califano's aides try to explain that the "illiterate and unskilled population" on welfare cannot be expected to work. But Carter does not buy this; he knows that within the welfare population there is a lot of talent and energy.

Eventually, a job creation provision is inserted in the welfare reform bill presented by Califano to Congress in 1978. The bill, though, never makes it through Congress. It has little momentum. It is pictured by conservatives as increasing government costs by $5 billion to $10 billion at a time when the priority is on government cost-cutting.

Califano concludes that his welfare reform is unsuccessful because welfare recipients are not a powerful constituency. But the story he tells points to another conclusion. Welfare reform fails because of Joe Califano's weaknesses. He is perceived correctly by Congress as a man who patronizes welfare recipients.

He regards welfare recipients as needing his protection rather than as having real abilities and as being worthy of the same expectations as others.

I don't want to be like Califano, I thought. I don't want to be one more liberal Washington lawyer, knowing nothing about how government programs really operate. The book, combined with the previous days' experiences, had led to a conclusion.

When the plane landed in San Francisco, I knew I would not be joining Berman's staff.

On the drive home at 11:00 P.M. I stopped at a light at Larkin and Grove. The driver of a yellow cab in the next lane called my name. I turned to see James Wonder, the first general manager of Renaissance Cleaners. He asked whether there was anything going at Renaissance; he was interested in running the Cleaners again. This is where I should be, I knew it.

There were times when I worried about being trapped in the nonprofit world. Among the men and women who operated the main antipoverty programs of the 1960s, many remained in San Francisco, but few had made a successful transition into private sector jobs. Some of the most prominent were looking for jobs. One man had been a high-ranking union official in the early 1960s and had served during the War on Poverty as an assistant in Washington to Sargent Shriver. He came to San Francisco to form a consulting firm in the 1970s when antipoverty consulting was big. In 1981 this consulting money largely was eliminated. In 1985 he came to Renaissance for a job. He had no skills valued in the private sector.

Yet, the Washington trip in early 1985 convinced me that the local level was the place to be, at least for the beginning of a career in public policy. I returned to Renaissance and to teaching at U.C. Berkeley, and I urged students, "Spend at least four to five years on the local level."

In Ignazio Silone's *Bread and Wine,* the recent university graduate Don Paolo seeks to use his reading and learning to improve the lot of the peasantry. But when he goes out into the villages, he is dismayed to find his learning and reading bear little resemblance to the grim realities,

Don Paolo went to his room to reflect on the peasants. . . and their lives. The idea occurred to him of using his remaining time at Pietrasecca to finish his essay on the agrarian question. He took his notebook from his bag and started reading the notes he had taken. He read them through and was astonished and dismayed at their abstract character. All these quotations from masters and disciples on the agrarian question, all these plans and schemes were the paper scenery in which he had hitherto lived.

Antipoverty policy over the past quarter century has been made in both Democratic and Republican administrations by persons with backgrounds as corporate lawyers and by legislative aides without backgrounds on the local level. Their illusions about the unemployed and the labor market have been proportional to their distance from local experiences.

And it has been these illusions that have so undermined the development of a strong and realistic employment policy.

Chapter 11

Christmas 1985 and beyond

"I sure don't miss the antipoverty world," Jay reflected as he talked of his new life in the private sector.

It was December 19, 1985, and Jay and I were standing together with Bill, Leon, and Don at the Renaissance Christmas party. The party was the one time when the various divisions of Renaissance came together, so there were the literacy students, participants in the Entrepreneurship Centers, the cable assembly crew, and the crew of Gold Mountain Courier, the messenger service. The party was running out of forks and spoons, and one of the messengers offered to go out for new supplies, but Don warned that with Gold Mountain Courier's track record we couldn't wait three days. The Reverend Jesse James stopped by, with a woman he introduced as his partner in a new restaurant business he was thinking about. "I've got plans."

Don made a presentation to Cathy Buckley, one of the early Renaissance graduates of the microcomputer class. Cathy had become a service manager for Computer MicroFinancial and had used her position to hire four other Renaissance graduates. This is what Renaissance is all about, Don explained, a family feeling. "Like a family, you're thrown in with people you'd never choose to be with, but you learn to love them."

Participants in past Renaissance training classes came by, and there were pleasant surprises. One of these was Anthony Johnson, who dropped out of the business machine repair class in 1982. I expected to hear Anthony say he had been in and out of jobs over the past year. Instead, he had worked as a sorter at a postal express company for nearly a year. He was referring his cousin Carlos, 17, to the Renaissance literacy classes. "I'm telling him that he has to take it a step at a time. Renaissance isn't going to help him unless he shows that he wants to help himself." "Unbelievable," was Don's comment. "Miracles never cease." My enthusiasm about Anthony's job stability, though, was dulled a little later in the party, when he disclosed he was earning only $4 an hour and looking around for something else.

Don was upbeat about Renaissance's prospects and planned to stay with the organization.

Look around the room today. Most of these young people would have gotten low-level jobs without Renaissance, but now they have jobs with a future, and they have accomplished something. Completing the course is the first time some of these young people have had a major victory, and that can be important no matter what they do.

I've seen inner city people who don't have the motivation, which is the key element; and I don't know what you do with them. Fortunately there are enough other inner city unemployed who do have the motivation and take advantage of training offered. I'd like to extend the Renaissance model throughout the nation, a Detroit Renaissance or a Chicago Renaissance. Come to think of it, I'd like to be in charge of the Hawaii Renaissance or Bahamas Renaissance.

In contrast to Don, the others—Jay, Leon, and Bill—were moving out of the job training world. "The antipoverty world is too dependent on foundations and government and too political," said Jay "I'm taking my luck in the private sector." After leaving Renaissance in January, Jay had joined a private planning firm, TEM Associates. The firm sought contracts with companies investigating areas for expansion and with local governments looking for economic development strategies. Over the previous six months, Jay had worked mainly on one contract with a rural county in northern California, examining the geothermal resources for horticulture and agriculture. But Jay expressed determination to stick with building his own firm. "My long-term goal now is to start a venture capital firm that will focus on new businesses through the private sector." Jay still saw new business development as the key for spreading ownership and creating jobs. "First, though, I have to make my own track record in the private sector."

Like Jay, Leon increasingly had become critical of the dependency of antipoverty groups and the behavior of foundations ("They like to fund something safe, like the symphony or ballet") and government officials ("None of them ever has operated a business"). Unlike Jay, he wanted to continue working at Renaissance, trying to devise entrepreneurial approaches. Did that mean developing new businesses, like the cable assembly or messenger service, for Renaissance and other groups? "Only partly. These businesses will never generate a great number of jobs. I want to experiment with new types of services, like care for the elderly or new forms of housing."

In 1982, when Renaissance was starting, Bill also was starting in the business world as a partner in Firehouse Barbecue restaurant. By 1984 this business had become his main activity. He served as chief operating officer and managed daily operations. By Christmas 1985 the business had grown to three restaurants in the nearby cities of Larkspur and Burlingame as well as San Francisco, with another planned to open in Santa Rosa. A total of 65 persons were employed.

I joked with Bill that he had created more jobs in the past three years than most antipoverty programs. He was serious as he explained his new interest in and respect for business.

When I graduated from college, profit was a bad word. I didn't want anything to do with business. But now that I'm running a business, I find I enjoy it. It's a real challenge, knowing you have a payroll to meet. Your employees know that they've earned their money every day.

I've grown to a new respect for business. Now when I hear a politician or 'community activist' say that we should make new demands on business, I no longer rush to support. I think policymakers must be more sensitive to business needs, because business primarily, and not the nonprofit sector, is generating wealth and jobs.

All policymakers should be required to operate a business before they tell businesses what to do.

The Yale community organizer had become a proponent of the free market system.

So had I. At Harvard in the early 1970s, I had been president of the Harvard Democratic Socialist Club. Strongly anti-Communist, the club favored the English Fabian socialism of R. H. Tawney, the Webbs, and R. H. S. Crossman, advocating greater government roles in industry and government planning. We often talked of the harshness of the free market and the need for an alternative system.

Over the next years, as I left college, I started to question these views, and the greatest break came during the years at Renaissance. One doesn't have to be long in the nonprofit and government worlds to be frustrated with the slowness of response, the lack of immediacy and efficiency in most transactions, the coming late to meetings. What a contrast to the vitality in much of the private sector, where drive and a sense of urgency often are present. The free market alone cannot generate sufficient jobs. But the free market vitality and drive is critical to an efficient economy that can truly reduce poverty.

The Monday after the Renaissance Christmas party, a Mr. Grieve came to visit Renaissance. Mr. Grieve was the president of Arrow Moving Systems, a moving company. He needed a new packaging division, to bid on a contract with the navy, and approached Renaissance Workers, a subcontracting operation we were forming. He talked of how we might join to submit the lowest bid: the workers' compensation costs, the transportation costs, the payroll taxes.

In the past, at Harvard or at Oxford, I would have considered Grieve to be boring and the conversation to be a dreary one. I would have contrasted it with exciting work done by government officials in the Department of Labor or by lawyers at the Senate Labor and Human Resources Committee.

Now I saw Grieve's work as exciting; he was building a business. Further, he was doing more in job generation than most of the government officials and Senate staffers. He was creating jobs for someone other than himself.

Renaissance continued to search for ways to generate new jobs, as well as ways to be more entrepreneurial in its training services.

By Christmas 1985 we had grown considerably from the initial 1982 operation of Jay, Silvia, me, and a few desks. There were now over 20 projects, including a variety of training programs, businesses, and five Entrepreneurship Centers stretching from San Jose to Oakland. Our training plans for 1986 called for a major program, Parents of Success, focused on training mothers on welfare. Parents of Success would help these women move off welfare and reduce repeat pregnancies outside marriage. It featured the intensive literacy training that had proved so successful in Tech Prep, as well as family planning, job placement, and follow-up for two years. It also featured an emphasis on avoiding pregnancies, at least until the woman became self-sufficient. "Are you trying to set behavior?" a foundation official asked. "Of course we are," I explained, "If these women are to concentrate on getting off welfare, they can't continue to have children in the next few years."

For our business development, we were adding only one new business in 1986, Renaissance Workers, a subcontracting business. The four existing businesses would be the main priority, along with the expansion of the Entrepreneurship Centers throughout the state and the growth of a seed capital fund for new businesses, Renaissance Ventures. We also were experimenting with job creation for job seekers in the mental health system and businesses involving residents of the housing projects.

Richard Thieriot the publisher of the main San Francisco newspaper, the *San Francisco Chronicle,* became chairman of the Renaissance board in November 1985 and pledged to generate business support. "Renaissance is a natural for business to become involved with; it doesn't seek one more government handout." To be sure, Renaissance had sought business support for three years with minimal results; but perhaps Thieriot could succeed. As publisher of the *Chronicle* (and owner of the NBC affiliate in the Bay Area) he knew everybody in the California business community. We looked forward to seeing whether he could convince business executives to do more than talk about unemployment.

"What should be done on a national policy level?" This was a question posed to us in 1985 by politicians and policymakers searching for "new ideas."

Sometimes I joked, "Give Renaissance more money." But by Christmas 1985 I no longer believed that a great outpouring of money to community groups, as in the 1960s War on Poverty, would have much effect in reducing inner city unemployment or poverty. The next U.S. War on Poverty would need approaches very different from those of the 1960s.

Chapter 12

The Possibilities for Job Training

An effective job training system is one of the approaches that will turn around our inner cities.

However, the needed training system differs significantly from our current one. This needed system injects entrepreneurial values—values of decentralization, creativity, and competition—into training. It opens the training process, allowing community-based training organizations to compete for training contracts against the public school systems and community college systems.

Further, the needed training system focuses a good part of its resources on the hardest-to-reach among the inner city unemployed and follows-up with training participants for years after initial placement.

The truths about our job training system are little evident in the publicized writings on inner city unemployment—the writings on both the political left and the political right.

For example, Michael Harrington's *New American Poverty*, taken up by the political left,[1] and Charles Murray's *Losing*

Ground, taken up by the political right,[2] have received wide notice and discussion recently. Yet, both are written very far from local experiences and bear little resemblance to realities in our inner cities.

During the 1950s, Michael Harrington worked on the local level among the poor (the first two years with Dorothy Day at the Catholic Worker in the Bowery). He was able to draw on these experiences in writing *The Other America,*[3] which stood out from so many books on poverty in its understandings of the people and conditions behind poverty statistics.

But in the years since, Harrington has done little daily work on the local level, and his newest book reflects this. His discussion of what should be done to reduce urban unemployment and poverty is limited to vague calls for a "full employment" budget and even vaguer calls for more "comprehensive planning."

As to the job training and antipoverty programs of the past two decades, Harrington does not question their effectiveness. Instead he pictures anyone who engages in such questioning as clearly uncompassionate and mean-spirited. Any shortcomings of such programs must be due to insufficient government money.

At the other end of the political spectrum, Charles Murray in *Losing Ground* does ask hard questions about past antipoverty programs, and his book is far more provocative than *The New American Poverty.* However, it is no more accurate a description of urban unemployment, nor is it valuable as a guide to policy.

Murray's main argument is that the antipoverty programs of the past two decades have hurt rather than helped the poor by creating a dependency. He includes job training programs among his targets, claiming that they have not helped the poor into jobs but in fact have undermined employment incentives and work orientation.

Murray first points to studies of job training programs showing limited earnings gains, below the anticipations of program
planners. However, the studies of earnings that Murray relies
on date back to the 1970s; and he ignores the considerable data
that have been gathered in the past decade.[4]

Murray presents a second, more subtle argument on the effectiveness of training programs: by their nature they induce a
dependency. According to Murray, these programs require for
entrance that a person be unemployed. They encourage persons
to be unemployed, to leave low- paying, entry-level jobs.

There is no question that labor market turnover is a major
element of inner city unemployment, as has been illustrated in
the first part of this book. But the presence of job training
programs is not the major or even minor causes of unemployment. Of the hundreds of persons who have come to Renaissance, it is difficult to think of one who left a low- paying job to
enroll in training. This is true throughout the job training system, especially since the training stipends of the 1960s and
1970s have been eliminated.

Moreover, job training programs are only one part of a publicly funded education system that includes state universities and
colleges and community colleges. Murray does not say why these
other institutions do not encourage the labor market turnover
that job training allegedly does.

Typical of Murray's quality of argument is his comment on
the favorable press coverage of job training:

The training programs lent themselves to upbeat anecdotes about individual success stories: John Jones, an ex-con who had never held a
job in his life, became employed because of program X and is saving
money to send his child to college. Such anecdotes, filmed for the evening news, were much more interesting than economic analyses . . .
Tacit or explicit, a generalization went with the anecdote: John Jones'

story is typical of what this project is accomplishing; depressingly often John Jones would be out of his job and back in jail a few months after his moment in the spotlight.

Murray has hit upon a major weakness of training programs: rarely do they include follow-up with participants for more than few days or months after training completion. However, Murray presents no job retention studies to support his argument; and in fact the retention studies do not support Murray's position.

Other recent critics of government job training programs, George Gilder and Edward Banfield, also fail to support their positions with data on training or understanding of local training programs.[5]

So what do the data on job training show?

The major nationwide studies on training available today cover primarily the period of the 1970s when CETA was in force. They fall into two major categories. One category of studies measures success in terms of earnings gains registered by participants over nonparticipants of similar socioeconomic characteristics.

Chief among these studies is "CETA Training Programs: Do They Work for Adults?" completed in 1982 by the Congressional Budget Office (CBO).[6] The CBO researchers found that earnings gains on the whole were limited, though there was a difference between women and men. Women in CETA programs increased earnings by $800-1200 per year, while men in CETA programs showed no significant gains.

The major data tool of the past two decades has been the Continuous Longitudinal Manpower Survey (CLMS) funded by the

Department of Labor. The CLMS has tracked training participants for a number of years after training completion. The CBO used CLMS information and focused on 1,615 female and 1,608 male participants over 24 years of age who entered training between January 1975 and June 1976 and stayed for at least seven days. Data for a comparison group of 21,096 women and 9,572 men was obtained from the March 1976 Current Population Survey. Wage information was gathered for 6, 16, and 36 months after program entrance.

The CBO found that for women, CETA increased average postprogram earnings by $800 to $1,300 a year. Of this increase, 80% was due to an increase in the amount of time worked. Among men no significant earnings gains were registered. After experiencing an earnings drop in the year before training, male participants returned to their more usual earnings levels after they left the program, with no gains over the control group.

The CBO researchers attributed the differences in gains between men and women to their different employment prior to training. The women worked fewer hours prior to training. They were in the labor force for 35 weeks on average during the year before they entered CETA training, whereas the comparative figure for men was 43 weeks.

The CBO researchers concluded that training programs were short-term (averaging 20 weeks in 1980) and relatively inexpensive ($2,400 per participant) and had some impact on participant gains, primarily due to an increase in the amount of time that participants worked. But this impact was not great enough to move participants very far above the poverty line or alter the distribution of income across the economy.

Professor Laurie Bassi of Georgetown University did an independent examination of the CLMS information, using a sample of CETA participants from 1976, and tracking them for two years after training completion. In a 1983 article, "CETA: Did It Work?" she summarized her findings, which were similar to those of the CBO researchers. The male participants showed no significant earnings gains in 1978 over nonparticipants. The women showed gains, ranging from $788 per year for white women to $1,145 for minority women. Professor Bassi further disaggregated the data by income levels prior to training. She found that the greater training gains were registered by the lowest-income participants.[7]

The CBO and Bassi studies, as well as the others on earnings comparisons, are good starting points in understanding the impacts of training. They indicate the limited macroeconomic effects of training in reducing poverty. Yet, these studies also have important limitations, particularly as they aggregate the more successful and less successful participants. Within the training population, a one-third or so of participants do not complete training or are not placed in jobs upon training completion, and in the aggregate data these "unsuccessful" participants disguise the substantial gains registered by another one-third of participants.

This becomes clear when examining a second set of CETA data that analyzes job placements. Between July 1974 and September 1981, 31,800 persons in San Francisco went through CETA training programs. Of these, 6,016 dropped out during training or were unemployed upon completion; 15,397 were placed in unsubsidized jobs, and 10,497 either continued into advanced training or entered the armed services.[8]

Nationally, direct job placements under CETA were slightly under 50 percent. The major form of CETA training was classroom training: participants attended classes in basic literacy skills or in such fields as secretarial, welding, word processing. Among classroom training participants, 41% were placed in jobs within a month after training. Another 30% went on to additional training (from say basic skills to word processing) or the armed services.[9]

Reviewing the many job training studies, Gary Burtless of the Brookings Institution in a 1984 article, "Manpower Policies for the Disadvantaged: What Works?" concluded that "these programs have not eliminated, or even substantially reduced, poverty among the working age population, but they have made a modest difference in the lives of many who participated in them." Burtless added,

"Proper training can occasionally turn a welfare mother into a computer technician. (In fact some welfare mothers will become computer technicians without any government aid.) But there is no magic training course that can guarantee every welfare mother self-sufficiency in a well-paid job."[10]

Additionally, Burtless examined the various approaches of training: classroom training, on-the-job training, work experience, wage subsidies. He found that the first two approaches showed higher earnings gains than the last two, but that between classroom and on-the-job training there was no significant difference.

Burtless and other researchers on job training have looked almost entirely to aggregate placement or earnings information. What of the individual training program? One of the few detailed studies of a training program was done in 1979-80 by Ken Auletta, a journalist. Auletta followed the progress of a training class in New York, both during the year of training and seven months after completion. His study is the finest reporting of job training of the past two decades.[11]

Auletta chose for his study the Wildcat Training Program, a New York site of the National Supported Work Demonstration. Supported Work, operating between 1974 and 1980, was one of the most ambitious training experiments. It focused on the inner city unemployed farthest outside the labor market: long-term welfare recipients, ex-offenders, ex-addicts, and young delinquents. Training sites were established in 15 cities across the nation. Supported Work participants attended classes to improve literacy and vocational skills and to learn the basic job search skills. They also were offered part-time jobs to gain work experience and income.

Auletta followed a class of 26 trainees attending Wildcat classroom training from December 1979 to June 1980. Only 10 of the 26 trainees completed the entire training course. Auletta writes,

Seven months in a classroom proved enormously frustrating to many. With the exception of Aubrey Powers, they were all high school dropouts. Many had earned more money on the streets than they received at Wildcat; their Wildcat salary barely exceeded the money they could receive on welfare. And there was no job guarantee at the conclusion of their year of supported work. Not seeing immediate results, not knowing if all these classes would lead to a job, many began to feel that they were being exploited, taken advantage of. "Many of our people were just getting out of the penitentiary or drug centers," Howard Smith (the instructor) said one day. "They weren't prepared for punctuality and attendance. They had just got half a foot in the work world. They're used to being in prison or at home with soap operas."

A number of the trainees drop out to take jobs, so that it is not clear whether their failure to complete the course should be considered a program failure. Among the training graduates, near all are placed in jobs, though seven months after graduation only seven of the ten are working. Three examples:

Willie Mason, the class valedictorian, wants to become a beautician, but he soon abandons this plan. Following graduation, he drifts between temporary jobs, until he finds a position as a private security guard for a public housing complex at $125 a week. By January 1981, seven months after graduation, he has been promoted to a lieutenant position, earning $161.50 a week.

Carlos Rodriguez is placed in a $150 a week cashier job through the training program, but leaves after a few months. He finds a second job as a clerical worker, but leaves this after a month, claiming "I had problems with people there and their attitude."

Denise Brown is unable to find a job for the first months after graduation, despite going to a variety of interviews. Then she finds a clerk-typist job at an insurance company, paying $131.35 per week. After five months, she is still on the job, with a $10 a week raise.

Willie Mason and Denise Brown are upbeat about program participation. Willie Mason says of the program, "They did a lot for me; They gave me a step back into society." Denise Brown adds, "I don't get depressed any more. I may get frustrated, but I've achieved a lot in the last two years."

Was the training worth the cost?

Auletta concludes that for 30 percent or so of the participants, the program not only placed them into jobs but significantly increased their confidence, work orientation, and long-term job prospects. On the other side, the cost per participant was over $6,000 (more than twice as expensive as most training programs). Auletta looks at various cost- benefit analyses but concludes that no formula can indicate whether this $6,000 expenditure is more worthy than other uses of government funds.

Auletta's observations of antipoverty programs of the past two decades have made him weary of large-scale government strategies. But he believes that a demonstration project, such as the National Supported Work Demonstration, that is carefully monitored and operated by community based organizations, does have a role. He concludes that inner city unemployment is distinguished by its complexity and the slow results that may be expected.

> The national demonstrations the MDRC has conducted among the underclass offer ample evidence of how difficult it is to reach those who figuratively reside at the bottom of society's barrel. There is no pink pill in this business. The MDRC's experiments suggest that progress is not measured by breathtaking touchdown passes, but by grinding out two, three, four yards at a time—Pearl Dawson, William Mason, Mohammed, Denise Brown, Hope Parker, Timothy Wilson.

Auletta's conclusions correspond to a great extent with our experiences in job training at Renaissance. A job training system, composed of well-run community-based training programs, can aid some of the inner city unemployed into jobs. Within three to four months a training program can teach unemployed persons the skills needed for such positions as telecommunications repair or office machine repair. It can teach job search skills— how to write a resume, how to behave at an interview, how to identify job openings—valuable throughout a work lifetime. It can set a positive, work-oriented environment and sometimes (with a dedicated and effective job counselor) can help the formerly unmotivated participant develop work incentive.

The Supported Work program placed only one-third of participants into jobs; but it trained the hardest-to-reach among the unemployed. Other effective community training programs are placing two-thirds of participants into jobs.

At the same time, the current training system is undercut by three key shortcomings: (1) an insularity and lack of competition; (2) a lack of tracking or follow-up after placement; and (3) too little focus on the hard-to-reach.

Injecting Competition and Market Orientation: In most large cities, the same organizations, many dating back to the 1960s, are funded year after year. The competition and new entries that produce increasing effectiveness in other fields of business are almost absent from job training.

I look back on the past four years of training in San Francisco (a city more open to innovation than most), and two scenes come to mind:

I'm at a meeting of the San Francisco Private Industry Council (PIC) in 1985. The PIC is the local body, composed of of employers and community representatives, that distributes the federal job training funds ($4 million for San Francisco in 1985-86). PIC collects proposals for training from local businesses and community organizations, evaluates these proposals and allocates funding.

Though the procedure supposedly is competitive, since 1981 the same community organizations have been funded year after year. At the 1985 PIC meeting, applying organizations appear and make a pitch for funding. The audience of 60 is composed mainly of staff of the long-funded training organizations, in attendance to protect their funds. Few in the audience or on the PIC committee are paying attention, for the process is a charade. A private for-profit business, not previously funded, talks earnestly of its connections to employers and new educational technology. But no one takes the speaker seriously, since the company previously has not been funded.

Renaissance's computer and office machine repair training receive high ratings from the training staff but are not recommended for funding. With no increase in federal training funds this year, priority has been given to previously funded agencies. Subsequently, we appeal the decision to the city council and win on an eight-to-three vote. But our success is due to politics, not program performance—no official really looks into our program performance.

Further, by the time of the city council vote I have spent 40 hours in meetings and lobbying (for a $40,000 contract). I wonder, Is this lobbying the productive work that I left law for? I'm certainly not creating any new jobs or training while sitting in the PIC meeting.

Later in 1985 the state of California announces the allocation of funds for "education clinics" to provide intensive reading and writing instruction for high school dropouts. The clinics are to work with dropouts to improve skills and direct them onto an educational track.

The Mission Reading Clinic, a local community based training agency specializing in literacy training for high school dropouts, applies to host a clinic. The reading clinic has built a record over the past ten years of teaching inner city teen-agers not reached by the public schools, and teaching at lower cost than the schools. But it is passed over, for the money is restricted to public school systems.

The insularity of our job training system will not be easy to break. Throughout the past 20 years, thousands of training schemes have been put forward to inject greater competition and entrepreneurism in inner city training and education. Few results have been achieved, for the existing training organizations and public school systems oppose these schemes, and the would-be reformers usually are worn down. Yet, if the politics are murky, the needed policy is clear. From the Department of Labor on down to state levels, the perception of job training agencies needs to change. These agencies need to be regarded, and to come to regard themselves, less as government agencies and more as entrepreneurial businesses. Operating in this fashion, they would worry more about costs and training placements and would search for ways of generating income beyond relying on government funds.

Training the inner city unemployed is not possible without some government funding. Neither private companies nor private foundations will provide anywhere near the financing needed for ongoing training operations.

However, community groups should be encouraged to complement government funds with selling services in the same way that private companies are expected to sell services. One example of this market orientation: community groups obtaining contracts with insurance companies. A second example: community groups obtaining contracts with private companies engaged in retraining displaced workers.

Entrepreneurial community-based organizations, competition, market orientation: these are key concepts for improving inner city training. They also are the key concepts for improving inner city public education.

Currently there are literacy programs operated by inner city training agencies that are showing dramatic improvement in the reading and math scores of at least a portion of high school dropouts. These programs tie literacy instruction to the main goal of most inner city young people: a steady job. They complement group classroom instruction with computer-assisted instruction. Their instruction is intensive.

These programs usually operate in a hand-to-mouth fashion, unable to compete for most public education funds. They should be allowed to compete against the public school systems for state and federal education funds.

Within most inner city communities, one-fifth or so of the teen-agers learn nothing, disrupt classes for others, and eventually drop out. The response of public school systems has been to try special classes or "alternative school" settings, usually with little success. It is time to look for approaches other than the public schools for these teen-agers, especially approaches that carry a job nexus.

Tracking trainees after placement: At the 1985 San Francisco PIC meeting to distribute federal job training funds, community organization after community organization stood up to claim placement rates of 80 or 90 percent of participants. In a number of these cases, the PIC staff countered that placement rates were closer to 40 or 50 percent; and debate followed. Yet, two key questions of training effectiveness were ignored: did the trainees stay in the jobs for more than a few weeks; and were they the hard-to-reach among the unemployed. Neither question is addressed well in training across the nation.

PIC's nationwide rarely track training participants for more than a month after training completion. There are good reasons for this. Tracking is very difficult, especially among a lower-income population that moves more often than the general population, has its phones disconnected more often, and is more suspicious of anyone asking questions. The result is that, after two decades of training, little is known of longer-term training impacts. The CLMS has provided tracking data for two to three years, but even this survey has been discontinued by the Reagan administration. Tracking by PIC staff of at least a sample of training participants would be worth the greater costs incurred, for it would provide important information on longer-term impacts.

On the other side, experimentation is called for with long-term follow-up measures by training organizations. For the past two decades, training organizations have seen their role as ending after job placement. Yet, the little tracking information that does exist indicates that initial placements do not ensure long-term labor market success. Can a training organization keep in contact with a trainee after placement, and, through individual and group support, improve job retention? It is an approach worth trying.

Greater focus on the hard-to-employ: The job training literature today is filled with calls for greater focus on the hard-to-reach among the unemployed. Yet, the training system continues to be structurally against reaching this group or honestly measuring outcomes.

To qualify for job training services, one needs be unemployed and low-income, as defined by federal guidelines. Though these guidelines are strict (less than $5,300 yearly income for a single individual, $13,120 for a family of four), within the eligible inner city unemployed population there is a scale of skills and motivations. At the upper end are the inner city unemployed who are motivated to get into jobs and who possess math and English skills above the eighth grade level. At the lower end are those such as Patrick Martin or James McFarland, whose skills are below the sixth grade level and who have not been able to hold a job.

There are good reasons why job training programs do not focus on this lower-end population: job placement rates are very low. James McFarland, for example, drops out of training despite intensive counseling, tutoring, and a part-time job. With

limited training resources, programs want to use these resources where they are likely to yield greatest success, with the unemployed who are motivated to work and need skills. In San
Francisco more than 40 percent of the training budget goes to
training programs serving immigrants, who are motivated and
seek English language training. These immigrant programs
show the highest placement rates.

Yet, this lower-end population, though small in number in
relation to the general population, constitutes a large part of the
inner city unemployment and crime at any time. Testifying
recently before a congressional committee, Gordon Berlin of the
Ford Foundation described the youth unemployment problem
mainly as "a relatively small group of mostly minority youth
with low education levels, who are frequently dropouts residing
in central cities." Berlin's description parallels that of Mitchell
Sviridoff, a former Ford Foundation official in charge of urban
programs, on the disparity between the small number of hard-
core unemployed and their destructiveness. "There is a segment
of the nation's poor, small and sometimes invisible, that does
not seem to be touched by...any traditional sort of out-
reach...Numerically this group is relatively small, but it is ex-
traordinarily destructive, and its behavior reflects intense
anger, with consequences on a scale that mocks its size."[12]

The National Supported Work Demonstration, established by
Sviridoff and chronicled by Auletta, was one of the few training
programs that focused on this lower-end population. As I have
noted above, the demonstration had less placement success—at
roughly 30 percent of participants—than other training
programs. But its limited placement, and the limited gains of
LUCD and other hard core programs, are great enough to jus-

tify continued experimentation with training in carefully monitored, honestly reported demonstration projects.

In April 1979, the *Washington Post* carried a series of articles on CETA programs. These articles portrayed CETA programs as having little impact other than income maintenance; and they noted that manpower experts remained in the dark about the nature of effective manpower strategy, particularly about how, if at all, the "structurally unemployed" could be trained and placed in jobs.

At the time I was completing law school and starting a temporary position as an attorney at the CETA agency in Hayward, California. I thought that this negative characterization of job training was inaccurate and was determined to set the record straight. During the next months I ran around to the various training programs in South Alameda County and sought out CETA participants. I wrote a lengthy reply to the *Washington Post*, arguing that training programs knew how to train the unemployed for jobs and mainly needed additional resources. Like many young writers coming to job training programs, I wrote in glowing terms of training success: Mr. X, who had drifted in and out of restaurant jobs until coming to the Advanced Training Center and being trained and placed as an electronic assembler; Ms. Y, who had been laid off from the Hunt-Wesson cannery and found employment after training as an electronics inspector.

Recently, in sorting through a series of files, I came across this reply and was struck by its ingenuousness (Did I write this?). Training program directors had told me of their placement rates of 70 or 80 percent, and I had taken their claims at face value. Like most journalists coming to the subject of training, I had avoided the hard questions of how long participants stayed in jobs and why many among the unemployed were not enrolling in training. .

Six years (and hundreds of training participants) later, I still believe in training as the bedrock of any effective antipoverty strategy. There are enough "successes," sometimes even with the least skilled or least motivated, to justify training, especially by community-based agencies.

But these years also have made clear that training alone will not reach Louise Allen or Anthony Johnson or James McFarland or hundreds of thousands of other inner city unemployed. Further changes in inner city incentive structures are called for.

NOTES — The Possibilities for Job Training

1. Michael Harrington, *The New American Poverty*, New York, Holt, Rinehart & Winston, 1984.

2. Charles Murray, *Losing Ground*, New York, Basic Books, 1984.

3. Michael Harrington, *The Other America*, New York, MacMillan, 1962.

4. Murray relies primarily on one study, Orley Ashenfelter's "Estimating the Effects of Training Programs on Earnings." This is one of the studies that tries to measure job training impacts in terms of the mean increases in earnings. The shortcomings of this approach have been noted earlier in this chapter. In fact, Murray himself recognizes the inadequacy of Ashenfelter's approach in footnote 38 of *Losing Ground*, explaining that a more informative statistic would be a measure based on the longer-term job experience of individuals.

5. George Gilder, *Wealth and Poverty*, New York, Basic Books, 1981; Edward Banfield, *The Unheavenly City Revisited*, Boston, Little Brown & Co., 1974.

6. U.S. Congressional Budget Office, "CETA Training Programs: Do They Work for Adults?" Washington, D.C., Government Printing Office, 1982.

7. Laurie Bassi, "CETA: Did It Work?" Washington, D.C., Georgetown University, 1984; Laurie Bassi, "The Effect of Direct Job Creation and Training Programs on Low-Skilled Workers," Washington, D.C., Georgetown University, 1984.

8. San Francisco Mayor's Office of Employment and Training, "CETA in San Francisco--Fact Sheet," San Francisco, 1979.

9. Robert Taggart, *A Fisherman's Guide: An Assessment of Training and Remediation Strategies*, Kalamazoo, Mich., W. E. Upjohn Institute, 1981.

10. Gary Burtless, "Manpower Policies for the Disadvantaged: What Works?" *Brookings Review*, Fall 1984.

11. Ken Auletta, *The Underclass*, New York, Random House, 1982.

12. U.S. House of Representatives, Subcommittee on Employment Opportunities, "Hearings on Youth Employment and Job Corps," Washington, D.C., Government Printing Office, 1984.

Chapter 13

The Possibilities for Inner City Work

In Washington today, and at universities throughout the nation, liberal politicians and writers have a clear idea of what needs to be done for the employment of Anthony Johnson, Louise Allen, and James McFarland. They don't need job training. They need to be given good jobs.

Economist Tom Larson of U.C. Berkeley summarizes this position in a recent article "Where are the Jobs for Young Black Men?" According to Larson, there is a severe shortage of jobs in the inner- cities, especially for inner city black youth. As Larson summarizes, "It is my view that blaming the victim is a waste of time—because high unemployment is due to factors largely beyond any individual's control. Rather, the lesson to be learned is that more must be done to provide jobs for blacks."[1]

What does it mean to provide jobs for black youth?

Larson does not say; and indeed it is difficult to find in any of the calls for more jobs an indication of how these jobs are to be generated. Among those who express such concern about the inner city unemployed, few have taken the time to examine the past government attempts to provide jobs, or to examine what it means to "provide" anyone with a job.

For the past two decades, government attempts to provide jobs for the inner city unemployed have been characterized by high costs per job, politicization of job distribution, and minimal impact on the long-term job success of participants. An exception has been the recently established conservations corps, though they serve primarily as training programs for a very small number of young people.

Anthony, Louise, and James certainly can be employed in our emerging economy. They need not be "superfluous workers." But their employment, like that of hundreds of thousands of others, is dependent on a series of changes in inner city incentive structures relating to expectations of and rewards for work. Chief among these changes are the rewards for good work in the entry-level jobs, the requirements of the welfare system, and the moral consensus to reduce teen-age pregnancies.

The conservation corps has been the exception among public jobs programs. Bob Burkhardt, the Executive Director of the San Francisco Conservation Corps, is accurate when he says of the public reaction: "They see our corps members, and they think, Something is going right in this country." Throughout America, local conservation corps have captured the public imagination, as they have set young people to work at public works projects, and as they have imposed strict discipline.

The vocational skills taught by the corps—building fire trails, painting and repairing buildings—may not be useful in urban labor markets. But the work orientation they demand—coming to work regularly, coming on time—is highly prized by employers. The corps serve as valuable training mechanisms.

But the corps will serve only a small number of inner city youth, for reasons of both economics and effectiveness. Only a few of the corps around the nation are able to generate income, through work contracts, and thus they are dependent on government subsidies. These subsidies amount to an average of $5,000 per participant in San Francisco, more than twice the cost of most inner city classroom and on-the-job training programs, and three times the cost of direct placement programs. The cost per corps member-year is $13,869. Further, the corps are effective precisely because they include the close supervision and emphasis on productive work that were absent from the 1960s Neighborhood Youth Corps and other government job creation efforts whose enrollments were greater. In San Francisco, Burkhardt believes that enrollment can increase to 500. However, this number still is less than one-tenth of the city's inner city unemployed (estimated at over 5,000). The San Francisco Conservation Corps currently enrolls 80-90 young people at any time, and it makes great effort to ensure productive work for this group.[2]

Apart from the conservation corps, government job creation of the past two decades has been the Neighborhood Youth Corps, Public Service Employment, and the Emergency Jobs Act of 1983. Chapter 9 has detailed the disappointments in hiring and work quality with these job creation attempts: the questionable work output of the Neighborhood Youth Corps and PSE, the few jobs and slow hiring of the Emergency Jobs Act. Chapter 9 also detailed the limited employment impact of these attempts. At a cost of $4.6 billion, the Emergency Jobs Act created 35,000 jobs, enough for only a fraction of the 8 million unemployed, while during the same time the private economy created 5.8 million jobs.

Government job creation sometimes is justified by politicians and writers not only for the immediate employment provided, but also for the value of job creation in helping the inner city unemployed gain work experience and move into other jobs. The inner city unemployed work in public service jobs and supposedly are able to move into private sector positions.

However, the placement data drawn from the largest public service job creation, PSE under CETA, undercut this justification. A leading researcher on training, Professor Laurie Bassi of Georgetown University, compared the earnings gains of CETA participants in the classroom training and on-the-job training programs against the gains of participants in PSE. She found the cost-effectiveness of the training programs was more than twice that of PSE.[3]

When PSE ended in 1981, there was hope that the participants would move into private sector positions. Yet, of 174,518 PSE workers laid off by June 30, 1981, the Department of Labor found that only 18% had moved into private sector jobs. Another 22% were collecting unemployment, and 15% were unaccounted for. Of the others, 25% moved into public sector jobs, 15% into other CETA training, and 5% into the armed services.[4]

Large scale public sector job creation as presently structured is not the answer for the unemployment of either Anthony, James, or Louise. This is a point worth emphasizing, for the idea of public employment has come into vogue. It has been taken up by policy analysts who see it as the solution to an otherwise uncontrollable situation in our inner cities.

For example, in late 1985, Nicholas Lemann, a white writer for the *Atlantic Monthly,* visited schools, businesses, and residences in the lower-income black area of South Chicago. He emerged deeply shaken by what he saw. After two decades of antipoverty efforts, he noted, the area was much worse than in the sixties. "By the sixties, when race relations had become a central national concern, the northern ghettos had received a large influx of migrants from the South, and they were portrayed as overcrowded, desperately poor slums stunted by racism. Today, after years of efforts to end poverty and discrimination, the ghettos are worse, much worse, than they were in the sixties."[5]

Lemann ascribed the worsening conditions in South Chicago to an underclass culture that had developed since middle-class blacks had moved out of the area, beginning with the passage of the civil rights laws. This culture attached little stigma to teen-age pregnancies and welfare support, and low priority to work orientation.

Lemann argued that the only way to break this underclass culture was to bring back a large-scale public works project modeled after the Works Projects Administration (WPA) of the 1930s. This new project would pay workers less than the minimum wage, so that private employment always would be more appealing. According to Lemann, the project would take young people out of their low-income areas and bring them physically and emotionally into the social mainstream.

Would Anthony, James, or Louise take jobs paying less than the minimum wage for public works projects? Not likely. Currently they and most other young inner city men and women who come to Renaissance will not take jobs paying the minimum wage. The San Francisco Conservation Corps, which pays minimum wage, is by no means inundated with applicants.

The difficulty of reaching high school dropouts with minimum wage jobs is shown also by the experience of the Youth Incentive Entitlement Pilot Projects (YIEPP) of the late 1970s. From 1977 to 1980 the federal government sponsored YIEPP, a major demonstration to test the effectiveness of job creation for inner city young people. YIEPP established operations in 17 cities, where low-income 16 to 19 year-olds who had not graduated from high school were offered minimum wage jobs, on the condition that they remain in school or return to school. There were 76,000 participants in YIEPP, at a government cost of $240 million. Information was carefully kept on job placement and education gains.

The results varied between these participants who were attending school at the initiation of YIEPP and the older ones who had dropped out of school. Those in a school, especially the blacks, showed very positive outcomes. Of these, 80 percent applied for the program, and 63 percent participated, figures that indicate their desire for work. Further, they held the jobs for substantial periods of time—on average participants worked 56 weeks at program jobs—showing their seriousness about work.

Yet, contrary to the hopes of program architects, only 25 percent of the the high school dropouts participated in the program. For this group, the unemployed young people of greatest concern to Lemann, the prospect of a minimum wage job was not sufficient to motivate either work or the additional schooling they needed to escape the low-wage jobs.[6]

Lemann can make his proposal for public job creation only because he does not bother to study the history of YIEPP or other public job creation. This type of program, particularly with low-wage, short-term positions, will not make any serious or long-term dent in inner city unemployment.

There are better approaches to spur achievement among inner city youth. In a short space below, it is possible to set out the broad outlines of these approaches, which operate primarily in the private sector, not public sector.

Imagine new scholarship approaches rewarding achievement in school or on the job. These scholarships would utilize market incentives to generate work and education.

A small indication of the power of market incentives to alter inner city behavior patterns comes from an experiment in New York City that brought dramatic results. In 1980 a wealthy entrepreneur, Eugene Lang, 66, returned to his former elementary school, P.S. 121, located in Harlem. In the midst of a rehearsed speech to the graduating sixth grade class, Lang announced that he would give each $2,000 toward college tuition, if they stuck with their books and finished school. Five and a half years later, with 12 months to go until high school graduation, 80 percent of the original 61 students still were in school—compared to a dropout rate of over 50% for other students from Harlem.

Lang kept in contact with students, encouraging them throughout the five-and-a-half-year period. Though his counseling was a factor, similar counseling has been present in other inner city programs. What Lang offered was more than words: he offered a financial reward and college opportunity. The idea of financial incentives can be expanded to include not only those for students to complete school, but also those for the unemployed to learn skills or to start in entry level jobs and advance.

A scholarship approach would possess three key characteristics: (1) incentives would go only to persons who had met performance standards; (2) they incentives would reward achievement on the job as well as in the classroom; and (3) they would be greater in size than the meager incentives now available.

The link to performance standards is primary. As Professor Lawrence Mead of New York University shows in his important new book on inner city welfare, *Beyond Entitlement*, the Great Society programs fell far short of the expectations of their architects.[7] Welfare recipients did not participate in the job placement offered to them, even though their actions were economically irrational: they would have been better off by working.

Professor Mead believes the roots of this behavior lie in the lack of expectations placed on welfare recipients. So long as persons could receive welfare without meeting any behavior standards, they did not develop the work habits needed for steady work. A better inner city incentive structure would link benefits to achievement. It would push persons to achieve. In Lang's experiment, the inner city young people were pushed to finish high school; the scholarships were dependent on achievement.

Inner city scholarships like Lang's reward classroom achievement. The principles of these scholarships, though, can be extended to rewarding and spurring achievement on the job, and they point to a way out of a key current dilemma of inner city young people moving in and out of the entry level jobs.

As has been evident in all Renaissance training experiences, most inner city young people are able to find entry level jobs. Anthony finds a job in a warehouse, James is employed at a restaurant and Louise works in an office. But they don't hold these jobs.

Even many of the hard core inner city young men sent for street or drug violations to the Youth Guidance Center, the juvenile detention facility in San Francisco, are able to find jobs. A project manager for employment programs at the Center who works with a hard-to-reach population of young men 17-21 years of age, explains:

"Contrary to what most people think, we are able to find jobs for most of our training graduates; the problem is that they do not stay in the jobs. After a month, fewer than half usually are at work." Counseling inner city young people on the importance of work or helping them to find other entry-level jobs (the approaches tried today to halt this work instability) have not yielded significantly greater work steadiness. This work steadiness will require an approach that focuses not only on job placement but also on job mobility. Anthony or James or Louise might stick in entry-level jobs for the same reason that other workers stick: if they can see a future.

Detailed research on job ladders is scarce (here is an area for the ambitious researcher). Bob Kuttner, one of the few economists willing to tackle this subject at the firm level, looked into job mobility at Blue Cross/Blue Shield, First National Bank of Boston, and Hewlett- Packard. He found that, even in these large firms, the opportunities to move up from entry-level jobs were limited and scarcer than in the past.[8]

At Blue Cross-Blue Shield in Massachusetts, approximately 4,000 persons were employed in 1983. Of these, 400 were rated managers, 1,000 were rated professionals (attorneys, actuaries, programmers, doctors, nurses), and 2,600 were rated clericals, including the entry level filing, sorting, mail delivery positions. Kuttner interviewed the manager of employee training who was not optimistic about promotion through the ranks, even for persons with good oral and written communication skills. As the manager described,

In the past, the lowest six levels of our clerical structure looked like an inverted pyramid. At the very bottom were jobs like filing, sorting, mail delivery, and basic data-entry jobs. You'd almost have to try not to be promoted in order to avoid rising through the clerical ranks. Most people did get promoted. With good oral and written communication skills, you could move fairly easily into a supervisory or junior management job. Those senior clerical jobs are disappearing, because the computer is taking over so much of the decision-making. We have a lot more routine jobs at the bottom, and a few more complex jobs at the top, where you need someone to analyze hundreds of pages of data.

At First National Bank of Boston, the nation's seventeenth largest bank, Kuttner found about 100 persons per year hired for the loan officer development program, an entry point for most managerial and executive positions in the bank. In 1983 fewer than 20 of the 100 persons were promotions from within, from the hundreds of teller and clerical workers. Instead, the future managers and executives were drawn from recent graduates of colleges and business schools. The 621 tellers earned an average of $6.59 an hour, or about $263 a week, and below them in salary were the backroom clerks and mail sorters.

At Hewlett-Packard, a manufacturer of computers and scientific instruments, Kuttner noted that the company prided itself on the "Hewlett-Packard way," a style of management with few barriers between the executive suite and shop floor. Yet, in this high-tech environment, Kuttner found a stratified system with the engineers, computer scientists, and executives on top, and the technicians and assembly workers below. Though movement was frequent from assembly worker to technician, the number of technicians was declining as the equipment became more self-diagnosing, and little movement occurred between technician and engineer.

Kuttner concluded from his findings of restricted mobility in the private sector that employment should be expanded in the public sector, where upward mobility was more prevalent. But another approach is possible: increasing mobility opportunities in the private sector.

Private firms will carve out this mobility if they have a financial motivation to do so. These firms will not act out of appeals to altruism. They will train and upgrade employees if, say, the costs of doing so are underwritten by a scholarship program.

Since the 1960s the federal government has sponsored on-the-job training for the inner city unemployed. Employers have received subsidies for hiring and training the unemployed. This training has been mainly for entry level jobs: the jobs as mail sorter, assembler, clerk.

The same principle can be used to reward achievement in entry level jobs, and to promote advancement from these jobs for both inner city and non-inner city participants. A work scholarship can be available to the entry-level worker who compiles an impressive work record for at least two to three years. The scholarship would be in the form of a voucher that could be taken to an employer, who would be reimbursed for training expenses. The size of the reimbursement would be related to the wage gain received by the scholarship holder.

The scholarship, at least initially, would be limited to workers earning less than $5.50 an hour. The mail clerk earning $4.50 an hour at Blue Cross/Blue Shield, for example, could apply for the scholarship after two to three years of steady work (at least one of these years with the same employer). The scholarship could be taken to Blue Cross/Blue Shield for training and advancement or to another employer. The employer would be reimbursed the training costs.

Focused on workers earning less than $5.50 an hour, the scholarship would not address the limited mobility from the bank teller position to the loan officer opportunities or from the technician position upward in the high-tech firms. These mobility issues would require other training or incentive structures. What the scholarship does offer is a way to address the work instability plaguing holders of the entry-level positions, especially inner city young people.

What would this work scholarship mean to Anthony or James or the young men coming through the Youth Guidance Center? It would mean incentive to build a good work record in the entry level jobs. It would mean the opportunity to develop skills in a dynamic employment setting.

"I believe that inner city youth today sense that they are not really needed in the work force. This sense may be on a conscious level or unconscious level, but I believe it lies behind much of the poor labor market behavior." The speaker was Gary Walker, 38, a vice president of a national job training organization, Public/Private Ventures, based in Philadelphia. Walker had graduated from Yale Law School in the early 1970s and joined a major Wall Street law firm. He left after two years to join the Vera Institute in New York and its programs to combat juvenile delinquency and inner city unemployment. He has operated and monitored a variety of employment projects and served as a senior vice president of the National Supported Work Demonstration during the late 1970s.

Walker has continued in the employment field for over a decade—resisting opportunities to return to law or to move to other more lucrative or glamorous fields. When we talked in 1985, he was excited about a project commissioned by the Ford Foundation to study the business generating possibilities of subcontracting by urban hospitals and universities.

However, his talk also expressed a pessimism about making serious inroads in reducing inner city unemployment. He had seen so many training programs over the past ten years. On an individual level, these programs showed "successes" in helping persons find work or long term jobs. At the same time, these programs seemed to be fighting against the tide against a labor market with fewer and fewer places for the inner city unemployed.

A concern that fewer and fewer jobs will be available in the United States has been present since the early 1960s. Automation then was eliminating positions in the manufacturing industries. What occurred, though, was that in the next 20 years new products developed, such as microcomputers and video cassette players, that created new jobs.[9]

New products and new jobs will continue to emerge. The work scholarship enables inner city young people such as Anthony, James, and Louise to be participants in this emerging economy rather than marginal outsiders.

It is pleasant to think that incentives alone will turn our inner cities around—pleasant but unrealistic. This thinking ignores that portion of the inner city population so lost in inertia and lack of confidence that they do not respond to work incentives. Louise Allen probably would respond to the work scholarship opportunities. Her two sisters and friend Patricia, all also on welfare, almost certainly would not respond. Their lives are so unstructured that only a requirement of work or training will break through their welfare dependency.

In 1981 the Reagan administration proposed that all state welfare systems require recipients to work in return for welfare. Congress rejected this proposal but did say that states could test a work requirement. By 1986, 37 states had enacted varying work programs for welfare recipients.

Though these work requirement programs all are in initial stages, the first results are positive. One of the first major programs was established on a trial basis in the city of San Diego, California in 1982. It included nearly 3,000 AFDC recipients, and its results indicate the promise of a work requirement.

The AFDC recipients were required first to attend job search workshops, to search for private sector jobs. The workshops featured one week of instruction in locating job openings, developing a resume, and behavior at interviews, followed by a two-week supervised search for jobs. Attendance at the workshops was high, and nearly 25 percent of the participants found jobs by the end of the workshops. Those unable to find jobs were then required to work in local government and nonprofit agencies. Most of the jobs were entry-level clerical or maintenance positions: operating copying machines, preparing files, helping to paint a public school. Though these jobs were not complex, the great majority of supervisors described the work tasks as necessary and the participants as comparable in skills to other employees.

The majority of participants regarded the work requirement as fair, and 60% said that their experiences would help them get a better job. When asked, "How do you feel most days about coming to work here?" 20% said they disliked the work, but nearly 70% answered that they looked forward to the work day.

Though the long-term employment impacts of the job experience were not measured, the short-term impacts were impressive, especially for the women with the longest times on welfare. According to the Manpower Demonstration Research Corporation (MDRC), this "worst off" portion of the welfare population showed both higher employment rates and higher earnings after their work experience than the welfare recipients in the control population.[10]

Similar initial positive impacts come from a welfare demonstration project operated by the County of Baltimore and monitored by MDRC.[11] Surveys of participants and supervisors found that the overwhelming majority of both groups regarded the work requirement as fair and the work as productive. The county gave incentive payments to participants who showed motivation and a positive work attitude, and over 70 percent of participants received these payments.

Surveying these and six other work requirement programs across the nation, Professor Richard Nathan of Princeton noted that the earnings gains of participants were not likely to be large. The jobs they usually obtained would pay around $5 an hour—not far above the poverty line. But the work requirement was important because it offered an approach to bringing welfare recipients into the work mainstream.[12]

This is an important point. The file clerk, retail clerk, receptionist jobs most available to welfare recipients do not offer quick relief from their economic struggles. But these job placements can be an important start, to the entire household.

The importance of a mandatory program goes beyond the value to the participant: it imposes a discipline and structure upon the welfare household. Talk to adults who work with the chronically unemployed and/or delinquent young people—police, teachers, job training directors—and the same story unfolds: these young people come from households where no parent works steadily, where no parent ever has worked steadily, where there is no structure or strong time orientation. As Eleanor Holmes Norton notes in a recent essay on reducing welfare dependency, "Jobs and training would augment self-esteem by exposing

women to the values and discipline associated with work, allowing them to pass on to their children more than their own dis-
advantages."[13]

Further, the work placements would heighten work orientation throughout the neighborhood. Professor Mead notes in
Beyond Entitlement that the number of men on AFDC is not in-
substantial at 18% overall, ranging among the states from 5%
to 46%.[14] These men would be covered directly by the mandatory
program. More important, though, the women, once working,
are less likely to be tolerant of unemployment among the men.

With all of these benefits, a work program for welfare
recipients would appear to be a sure policy reform. But the op-
position from church and legal aid organizations has been considerable. In 1985 in California the Friends (Quaker)
Committee on Legislation, the American Civil Liberties Union,
the Western Center on Law and Poverty, and ten other "public
interest" groups joined to oppose a proposed work program for
welfare recipients. Fortunately, this work program, the Greater
Avenues to Independence (GAIN), was enacted, it required welfare recipients to participate in training or work. But the battle
over GAIN was a telling one.

On the day of the State Senate hearings, the "public interest"
groups bused welfare recipients to Sacramento to oppose GAIN
as forced labor. State Senator John Garamendi, a proponent of
GAIN, encountered a group of the welfare recipients in the
hallway. Garamendi recalls, "These women had been told that
they would be kept in subminimum wage positions. When I explained that the work placements and training were aimed at
moving them into regular jobs, their attitude changed; they had
been tricked by the protest organizers."

On the day of GAIN's enactment, an NBC television crew interviewed a San Francisco "public interest" lawyer who denounced GAIN as constituting involuntary servitude. Then the crew went to the city's Department of Social Services to interview welfare recipients. What a dramatic difference. "Nobody has been willing to hire me," one middle-aged woman commented "I want an opportunity to do something, to get out of the house."

The creation of public sector jobs that offer this woman and others on welfare more than the busywork of past government job creation will not be easy. Also, structuring child care arrangements that are effective and do not bring enormous costs or bureaucracy will call forth creative private sector responses. But the effort is well worth the benefit: a possible breakthrough in reducing welfare dependency.

A further breakthrough in reducing welfare dependency lies beyond economics in a stronger moral consensus to reduce teen pregnancies.

This may seem obvious, but a consensus is far from present today, especially among the social workers, foundation officials, and job training staff who work with low income teen-agers. These youth professionals are uneasy with questioning the "right" of a teen woman to have a child. They prefer to talk about nutrition or prenatal care, and not about the choice to have a child. They resist saying what must be said: that it is wrong for a young woman to have a child and expect the state to foot the bill.

"The difference between the inner city teen-age women who have children out of marriage and turn to welfare and those who do not, is that the latter have an agenda; they see a future for themselves." This observation is made by nearly everyone con-

nected with inner city unemployment—job counselors, probation officers, school officials.[15]

Job training programs can help some of these young women
and men to build this agenda. But a teen woman with child raising responsibilities as a single parent (especially with more than
one child) faces an uphill training and job career path. Further,
even if training were more successful than it is, the economic incentives need to be augmented by moral sanctions.

Looked at individually, Anthony, Louise, and James, are all
difficult to dislike or to be angry at. Yet their lives are going
nowhere, and their lack of work is an economic drain on the nation.

In a widely read 1985 *Commentary* article, "Helping the Poor:
A Few Modest Proposals," Charles Murray elaborated on his arguments in *Losing Ground.*[16]

Liberals and conservatives alike, are indulging themselves when it
comes to the problems of poverty, ... The nation is faced with some
critical social pathologies that are not going to be solved or even much
changed by a continuation of present policies. The moderate fixes and
the fine-tuning will make us feel we are doing something. They will
provide work for the program evaluators for a few more years. And
each time we stop to take measure, it will be found that the problems
are just as bad as they were a few years earlier.

Murray goes on to put forward a variety of dramatic changes
in our poverty approaches, ranging from paying teen-age women
not to have children to residential poorhouses. Murray's policy
solutions, like other dramatic solutions such as eliminating welfare or taking away the right to vote from welfare recipients,
represent hysterical responses to inner city unemployment

rather than any serious understanding of it. Yet Murray is correct on one score: greater work expectations must be held for the inner city unemployed than liberals and even many conservatives have been willing to hold in the past.

NOTES — The Possibilities for Inner City Work

1. Tom Larson, "Where Are the Jobs for Young Black Men?" *California Tomorrow,* Fall 1986.

2. An independent assessment of the San Francisco Conservation Corps was commissioned by the Ford Foundation in 1985 and urdertaken by the Public/Private Ventures research group, based in Philadelphia. The interim report, issued in April 1986, praised the close supervision and emphasis on productivity. However, it noted that the strict corps rules, while building work habits among some young people, also lead to a high turnover rate. Public/Private Ventures, "Youth Corps Case Studies: The San Francisco Conservation Corps," Philadelphia, Public/Private Ventures, 1986.

Studies of other corps include Public/Private Ventures, "The Califonria Conservation Corps: A Report on Implementation," Philadelphia, Public/Private Ventures, 1985; and Public/Private Ventures, "Youth Corps Case Studies: The Canadian Youth Corps," Public/Private Ventures, Philadelphia, 1988. The Canadian corps had slots for 1,584 youth in 1985-86. Participants were volunteers, though they received a $1,000 "honorarium" at the end of the nine-month program.

3. Laurie Bassi, "CETA: Did It Work," Washington, D.C., Georgetown University, 1984; see also Laurie Bassi and Orley Ashenfelter, "The Effect of Direct Job Creation and Training Programs on Low-Skilled Workers," Washington, D.C., Georgetown University, 1984.

4. "Business Slow to Hire from CETA, Frustrating Reemployment Plans," *Wall Street Journal,* September 17, 1981.

5. Nicholas Lemann, "The Origins of the Underclass," *Atlantic Monthly,* June 1986, July 1986.

6. A fine summary of YIEPP results is contained in Judith Gueron, "Lessons from a Job Guarantee: The Youth Incentive Entitlement Pilot Projects," New York, Manpower Demonstration Research Corporation, June 1984; see also George Farkas et al, "Post-Program Impacts of the Youth Incentive Entitlement Pilot Projects," New York, Manpower Demonstration Research Corporation, June 1984.

7. Lawrence M. Mead, *Beyond Entitlement,* New York, Free Press, 1986.

8. Robert Kuttner, "The Declining Middle," *Atlantic Monthly,* July 1983.

9. James Fallows, "America's Changing Economic Landscape," *Atlantic Monthly,* March 1985.

10. Barbara Goldman et al, "Preliminary Findings from the San Diego Job Search and Work experience Demonstration," New York, Manpower Demonstration Research Corporation, 1984.

11. Janet Quint, "Interim Findings from the Maryland Employment Initiatives Programs," New York, Manpower Demonstration Research Corporation, 1984. For other initial findings on state work/welfare initiatives, see "Interim Findings from the Arkansas WIN Demonstration Program," New York, Manpower Demonstration Research Corporation, 1984; Joseph Ball, "Interim Findings on the West Virginia Community Work Experience Demonstrations," New York, Manpower Demonstration Research Corporation, 1984.

12. Richard Nathan, "A Welfare Revolution," *Washington Post,* April 10, 1986; Richard Nathan, "New-Style Workfare—It Could Be the Real Welfare Reform," Princeton, N. J., Princeton University, Department of Economics, 1986.

13. Eleanor Holmes Norton, "Restoring the Traditional Black Family," New York Times Magazine, June 2, 1985.

14. Lawrence Mead, *Beyond Entitlement,* New York, Free Press, 1986.

15. For example, in early 1984, Joe Klein, a reporter for *New York* magazine looked into teen mothers and welfare in New York City. Nearly 15,000 teenage women per year gave birth to children in New York City, and a study by the city council president found nearly 70% of these women on the welfare rolls within a year. Reflecting the views of others interviewed, Al Moran, the head of Planned Parenthood in New York commented, "The kids who have abortions are the ones with an agenda. They want to go to college, they have a career in mind, and they have plans, goals. The kids who have the babies tend to live in a vacuum, passive, submissive, without hope. So the key factor isn't race, it's hope." Another counselor with pregnant teens commented to Klein, "There's a glamour to being pregnant, a celebrity status. Suddenly you're the center of attention. The really sad thing is that once the baby is born, the party is over." Joe Klein, "Babies Having Babies," *New York,* February 6, 1984.

16. Charles Murray, "Helping the Poor: A Few Modest Proposals," *Commentary,* May 1985.

Chapter 14

The Possibilities for Inner City Entrepreneurship

The Mission district, as a low-income inner city area, has been the object of federal and local antipoverty efforts over the past two decades. Few of these efforts have had discernible impacts, at least in creating jobs or economic activity. Yet, over the past five years, new business growth has surged in the Mission. Walking down the main street, Mission Street, from 16th Street to 24th Street, one sees new retail outlets, restaurants, produce stands, auto repair shops.

The primary reason for this business growth is not any government program. Rather, it is the result of decisions by private entrepreneurs, especially Asian-Americans. These entrepreneurs are starting businesses and generating new jobs.

The Mission district indicates the key role played by private new small businesses in revitalizing inner city areas. It is a role that can be expanded greatly throughout the nation, if only we can recognize the need for new policies of inner city financing, entrepreneurship centers, and reduction of government regulation.

The data on job growth in urban centers is startling in the main role played by new businesses. In nearly every urban center around the nation, new small businesses are generating the majority of new jobs.

The path breaking work in the study of job generation was done in the 1970s by a research team at the Massachusetts Institute of Technology. Led by Professor David Birch, the researchers sought to look behind the aggregate employment data, to determine the characteristics of firms that generated most jobs. Using Dun and Bradstreet data on business growth and demise in the early 1970s, they analyzed job growth by size and age of firm.[1]

The main generators of jobs were not the large, established firms, but new business start-ups. Small firms, defined as those with fewer than 20 employees, were responsible for more than 65% of new jobs. New firms, defined as those less than four years old, were responsible for more than 75% of new jobs.

Further, Birch examined cities of strong job growth, such as Houston, and cities of weak job growth, such as Rochester and Dayton. The difference between these cities was not in business terminations: in all of them more than one-fourth of firms ceased operations in the five year period between 1972 and 1976. Instead, the difference was in the start-ups. In Houston, while firms were closing, more than enough other firms, an amazing 62.7% were opening. In contrast, in Rochester the gain new firms was only 33%.[2]

San Francisco entered the 1980s as a business headquarters city, with the headquarters operations of over 50 major U.S. companies, including Bank of America, Wells Fargo Bank, Transamerica, Crown Zellerbach, Natomas, Pacific Telesis, and

Chevron. The years 1980-84 actually saw a loss of jobs among these and other major companies. During these years, firms in San Francisco with 100 or more employees posted a net loss of 6,107 jobs. The local economy was saved by small firms, which created 8,660 jobs.

Most of these job generators were new business start-ups. Firms less than four years of age created 28,616 jobs, while all other firms combined actually lost 25,803 jobs.[3]

New businesses are arising and generating jobs in urban areas across the nation. Another example: the Denver/Boulder economy grew by a net of 76,993 jobs between 1980 and 1984. Firms of fewer than 20 employees created 39,972 jobs, more than half of the total. More dramatic is the breakdown of job creation by age of the firm. New business start- ups, defined as firms less than four years old, created 93,750 jobs, while all other firms lost a total of 16,757 jobs.[4]

A reporter on assignment from *Inc.* magazine in 1986 examined inner city areas in Los Angeles, Atlanta, and Miami, and found a number of these areas bustling with economic activity.[5] The reporter was excited about Los Angeles, exclaiming,

"Hispanic East Los Angeles, Chinese Monterey Park, and Koreatown, on the edge of downtown are all bustling with new and growing businesses, both retail and manufacturing. There is noise and congestion; signs in a potpourri of languages compete for your attention."

In Miami's Little Havana and Hialeah, the reporter marveled at "the bustling garment factories, coffee shops, trading firms."

Still, there are inner city areas lagging behind in new businesses, especially in city black areas. The *Inc.* reporter contrasted the business activity of the Cuban areas of Miami with the "economic torpor" of black Liberty City and Overton and described the "attitude of abandonment" of black sections of Watts and South Central Los Angeles. "Many of the storefronts are vacant. The manufacturing firms that survive employ Asians and Hispanics. The commercial life consists of little more than liquor stores, franchise restaurants, and bars—and increasingly even these are falling under ownership by Asians and other outsiders."

Indeed, throughout the country, blacks have lagged behind both whites and other minority groups in starting new businesses. The most recent Census Bureau Survey of Minority Owned Businesses showed blacks owned about nine enterprises per 1,000 population, a rate about half that of Hispanics and one third that of Asians. Among self-employment rates, blacks were at a low 3.09% in 1980, compared to 5.25% for Hispanics, 7.7% for Asians, and 12% for whites.

Why has black entrepreneurship been so limited? When black business persons and scholars are asked this question, they generally cite two factors: (1) the lack of an entrepreneurial tradition similar to the tradition in other ethnic communities; and (2) the lack of a group relation of blacks buying from black businesses.

Robert Hill, a black historian at the University of California, Los Angeles, traces the lack of an entrepreneurial tradition to the communitarian societies of Africa, and to the lack of business opportunities open to blacks in the United States, even after Emancipation. The low rate of business activity of American blacks is contrasted by historians with the higher rate of business ownership by blacks from the West Indies, who had opportunities for business ownership in their native land (and whose median income now exceeds the median income of American whites). Other black businessmen speak of the lack of status given to the entrepreneur, in contrast to the black ministers, teachers, doctors and lawyers. When the civil rights movement of the 1960s opened new jobs and opportunities for blacks, the talented mainly went to work in mainstream businesses and government; few opted to start businesses. "A lot of my black classmates at Harvard felt they were getting the opportunity we never had before", explains the president of a family-owned construction firm in Atlanta.

Tony Brown, host of a series for public television, points to the lack of a group purchasing loyalty among blacks, like the loyalty that exists in the Chinese, Jewish or Cuban community:

"The Chinese are helping the Chinese, the Haitians help the Haitians, Cubans help Cubans, but blacks are helping everyone else. We have been conducting the most successful business boycott in American history—against ourselves." A Cuban banker in Miami agrees. He notes that Miami's Hispanics control 30 banks, while only one small bank in South Florida is black-owned. He continues,

"If a Cuban had a cleaning shop and we knew him, we lent him money. And people in the community bought from that store because the owner was Cuban. Blacks have to do the same. They have to help themselves, their own people."

At the Renaissance Entrepreneurship Center, the entrepreneurs did not differ sharply along racial lines: among all racial groups there was a mixture of promising and unrealistic participants. But on the whole, the aspiring black entrepreneurs did have weaker networks of family and friends to support their ventures, far less capital, and less individual and family experience in entrepreneurism than the other entrepreneurs, especially than the Asian entrepreneurs. And after the first year while the white, Asian, and Latino entrepreneurs showed some growing businesses, the black-owned businesses all were struggling.

Chapter 8 recounts the business experiences of Entrepreneurship Center participants and the difficulties they encountered in starting businesses. Two of these experiences worth expanding on are those of Bill Walker and R.C. Monceaux. Walker, 35, was a bus driver, who had started a photography service, which he hoped to expand into his full-time occupation and on which he spent all of his spare time and all of his spare money. His partner, Andre Taylor, 36, was a paraplegic, who was trying to make a go of the business full-time. After meeting them at a center gathering, my wife Donna commented, "If there's any fairness in the world, those two will succeed."

But they were not succeeding. They bid for corporate and city contracts and constantly were turned down. They offered their services free on a trial basis to *Black on Black Singles*, a publication aimed at Bay Area black singles, but the services never led to paid work.

In January 1986, Donna and I received an invitation to a Saturday night showing of Walker/Taylor photographs at the Black Like Me Gallery on Hayes Street. This is a break for them, I thought, since Hayes Street was an up-and-coming area of new galleries near Civic Center. When we arrived, though, the "gallery" turned out to be a fourth-floor private apartment in the run-down section of Hayes Street out toward Golden Gate Park. The photographs, numbering eight, hung on the walls. Ten or eleven men and women were gathered talking and drinking in the living room, none appearing to have the slightest interest in the photographs.

The owner of the apartment was a black man in his early thirties, who introduced himself as R. C. Monceaux, the proprietor of the Black Like Me gallery. He envisioned the gallery as "a major showplace for black art in the Bay Area." He wanted to run the gallery full- time, to be a full-time entrepreneur. Unfortunately, he hadn't made many major sales in the past year. The paintings were listed at $400 or $500 each, well above what the 12 people partying in the room would pay. Monceaux was continuing his job as a mechanic.

Should the government provide any greater assistance to entrepreneurs like Walker, Taylor and Monceaux? Is there any assistance that can be provided?

In the 1960s and 1970s the federal government thought that the development of businesses by inner city entrepreneurs could be spurred by access to capital. Loan programs were launched under the Small Business Administration (SBA) and Economic Development Administration to finance new businesses owned by blacks or located in inner city black areas. Other financing programs for inner city businesses were operated by consortia of private banks.[6]

Loans to businesses were made, but many of these were not repaid. Loan loss rates soared above 30 and 40 percent, far higher than average bank loan loss rates.

Reliable data on repayment rates is scarce among these loan funds, but two that were subjected to independent study were the SBA's Minority Loan Portfolio, and the Job Loan and Urban Venture Corporation of Philadelphia. Both showed loan default and delinquency rates of over 40 percent of loans.

The SBA started a more aggressive policy of minority lending in 1967. It established the Economic Opportunity Loan program targeted at low income and minority entrepreneurs.

As a financial economist with the SBA, Richard Klein was able to gather records of the 49,782 minority loans made between July 1967 and June 1976. At the time in late 1976 when Klein did his analysis, 27,272 loans were still in servicing with no clear results on repayment. Among the remaining loans, 38% (9,060) were paid in full, and 62% (13,450) were either charged off or in liquidation. In contrast, 126,389 non-minority loans were made during this period, of which 78,116 were still in servicing. Among the remaining loans, 72% (35,123) were paid in full, and 28% (13,150) were either charged off or in liquidation.[7]

Noting the substantial differential in loan loss rates, Klein criticized SBA officials for rushing to fund many minority entrepreneurs not prepared to start enterprises. These entrepreneurs lost not only the SBA funds but usually at least an equal amount of their own funds. Klein urged that funding be tied more closely to business training prior to business start-up and to more hard-headed evaluations of business success.

The Job Loan and Urban Venture Corporation (JLUVC) of Philadelphia was created in April 1968 by eight Philadelphia commercial banks to issue and guarantee loans to minority entrepreneurs. Between April 1968 and January 1970, JLC processed 848 applicants, of whom 290 were approved for approximately $3 million in loans.

Professor Robert Edelstein of the University of Pennsylvania was able to obtain data on the status of the 290 loans as of January 1970. Only 42% (122 loans) were current in payments; 17% (48 loans) were less than two months behind in payments; and the remaining 41% were either more than two months behind (79 loans) or written off (41 loans).

Edelstein was critical of JLC for not utilizing professional standards in granting loans, relying instead on friendships and good intentions. Later he criticized the participating banks for abandoning JLC instead of sticking with it and trying to overcome the initial shortcomings.[8]

The majority of privately financed loan funds launched during the 1960s were abandoned because of disappointing loss rates.[9] Among those abandoned was the Opportunity Through Ownership Fund in San Francisco, established by Bank of America, Wells Fargo, and other local banks. When Renaissance approached these banks for investment in a new inner city loan fund in 1986, we met repeated rejections and the explanation, "The bank tried this type of loan fund in the sixties and seventies and suffered huge losses."

The idea of inner city loan funds has not been abandoned entirely. Quietly, in recent years new inner city and minority funds have arisen. These funds have shown considerably greater success in repayment rates than past funds. They suggest new directions in inner city financing.

Three examples of these new loan funds are the Oakland Business Development Corporation, Coastal Enterprises in Maine, and the Community Initiatives Consortium in St. Paul, Minnesota.

- The Oakland Business Development Corporation (OBDC) was launched in 1979 to stimulate new businesses in Oakland, especially those that were minority owned or hiring from the low income unemployed of Oakland. Capitalized with nearly $1 million of city funds, OBDC's first years followed the disappointment of earlier loan funds, with decisions made by community representatives, inexperienced in banking, and loss rates reportedly over 35% of loans. In 1982 the city restructured the loan committee to include primarily banking professionals. A

Bank of America loan officer was brought in to be
executive director.

From November 1982 to November 1985, OBDC made
32 loans to small businesses, mostly loans in the range of
$10,000-$50,000, with three-to five-year repayment
schemes. In November 1985 only 3 of the loans were in
default, with another 3 between 30 and 60 days past due.
The remaining 26 loans were either paid off or on schedule
in repayment.

• Coastal Enterprises is a private nonprofit corporation,
headquartered in Wiscasset, Maine and financed with
private capital from the Ford Foundation, Union Mutual
Life Insurance, and various churches. It targets both
start-ups and expanding businesses that are unable to
obtain other institutional financing and that agree to hire
from the low-income unemployed population of the area.
Firms that receive loans from Coastal Enterprises sign an
employment training agreement pledging to hire when
appropriate from the welfare recipients and jobless.

Between 1979 and 1985, Coastal Enterprises financed
35 ventures, primarily manufacturing and wood product
firms and fisheries, with most loans in the range of
$25,000-$75,000. By late 1985, 30 of these loans were
either repaid or current, with only 5 more than 90 days
past due.

• The Community Initiatives Consortium in St. Paul was
started in 1981 by nine local life insurance companies and
financed with private funds. The consortium targeted
minority-owned businesses and businesses that would be
main job generators. Between 1981 and 1984, 24 loans
were made to ventures such as bakeries, cleaning services,
and construction contractors. By fall 1985 only 2 of the
ventures had defaulted on loans, with 6 other ventures
delinquent from one to three months. The remaining 16
loans were repaid or on schedule in repayment.

Traveling across the United States, one finds other new inner city and minority loan funds avoiding the mistakes of the past two decades and, though in their initial stages, showing low loss rates. Central to the success of these new loan funds is the business approach they are taking. Though they are willing to take greater risks than the private banks today, they hold applicants to higher standards of business feasibility than did the past loan funds. They utilize professional criteria in decision making, carefully monitor loans, and require the participation of other private financing sources.

Professional criteria in decision-making: By professional criteria is meant the factors of business promise widely used by private lending sources. "In the first years, our loan committee was made up of lay persons who loaned money to nearly anyone who sounded sincere," notes the OBDC executive director. "Now, with our committee of banking professionals, we look for the applicant's experience in the field, the applicant's capital injection, and a convincing business plan."

The Massachusetts Community Development Finance Corporation (MCDFC) is another of the new loan funds. It started with a community oriented loan committee and, like OBDC, has adopted a more professional approach. MCDFC is a state-sponsored fund, capitalized by a $10 million general obligation bond in 1979. In its first years, MCDFC invested heavily in businesses operated by community-based organizations, and it suffered default rates of over 40 percent. In the past few years, a new management team has been brought in with a mandate to evaluate financing requests with a stronger emphasis on business feasibility and less on community good intentions.

"We do a thorough credit review," says MCDFC vice-president Nancy Nye, "studying the product, the competition, the management capability. We also have improved our deal flow, so we are able to choose among a greater number of applicants." Since 1982, MCDFC has made loans to 25 business ventures. Of these, 18 are current, and 3 have been paid off.

Renaissance added a revolving loan fund, Renaissance Ventures, in late 1985, to finance ventures by Entrepreneurship Center graduates. Through the first six months, it made 11 loans. Although these have been "micro loans," in the range of $2,000 each, they have enabled recipients to buy computer equipment and marketing materials and to obtain other financing.

Leon Willard directs Renaissance Ventures, and he comments on the need for a professional review of the business. "There is no clear test for judging whether a new inner city business will succeed. Some entrepreneurs who break all of the rules of good business management manage to succeed. But to finance an aspiring entrepreneur on the basis of wanting to succeed, rather than careful assessment, is not doing the entrepreneur a favor."

Close monitoring of loans: "We keep our loan numbers small so that we can closely monitor each one, and offer any management assistance needed," explains Ellen Golden, the operations manager of Coastal Enterprises. Coastal Enterprises requires each of the ventures funded to submit financial statements on a periodic basis. If a venture shows financial difficulties, Coastal Enterprises staff or consultants will provide assistance in marketing or management.

The other loan funds also emphasize monitoring. Like Coastal Enterprises, they are able to do so because their portfolios consist of fewer than 20 new loans a year and because technical assistance is built into their structure. "We see ourselves not as a bank, which takes a passive role in investment," notes Leon

Willard, "but as a venture capital firm, stepping in with strategic planning when needed."

Participation of other private financing sources: Most of the new loan funds have moved away from being the sole or even the major source of financing. For example, MCDFC will provide financing for only up to one-third of the total financing needed, requiring applicants to secure other private resources. The involvement of other private sources provides additional review of business plans, and it enables the loan funds to leverage their participation. "With a loan from us, the entrepreneur is in a better position to approach other private lending sources," adds Ellen Golden of Coastal Enterprises.

In short, the new loan funds do not treat the loan monies in the way that past loan funds often did, as government grants that can be spent with little accountability. Rather, they act as private financiers, as bankers or venture capitalists, who know their own jobs and future are tied to the performance of the fund.

These new funds, grounded in business realities, are one important way of stimulating inner city business growth. A second way is through inner city entrepreneurship centers that provide mini business school training and group camaraderie.

These centers cannot ensure business success; they cannot provide the marketable ideas and resilience needed for business success. But they can help aspiring entrepreneurs stay out of businesses in which they are likely to fail, help develop basic marketing, finance and management skills, and help avoid the isolation that can demoralize beginning entrepreneurs.

Joyce Burris comes to the Renaissance Entrepreneurship Center planning to start a bed and breakfast inn, with no experience in the field and no way of raising the $200,000 that she anticipates is needed. Through the center she is led to another business idea, computer programs and services for law firms, far more in line with her experience and capital resources. Armando Zelaya is inspired to turn his part-time house-painting efforts into a business that markets and grows to hiring others. Even Greg Richardson, a sporadically employed longshoreman, stops jumping from business idea to business idea, completes a business plan, and starts a business offering typing and filing for offices. These are small victories, to be sure. But they can be multiplied, as entrepreneurship centers are started in inner cities across the nation.

These centers, combining a four-month training in the skills of new business development with individual follow-up, will differ sharply from the "business assistance" strategies that the government now funds in inner city communities. These strategies often consist of hiring business consultants to go into inner city businesses and advise them how to operate more effectively.

The results always are difficult to measure, other than creating jobs for the consultants. In contrast, the centers enable the entrepreneurs to develop their own skills and follow up with assistance over a period of years. Though the centers maintain a paid staff, salaries are kept modest so that any government funds can reach the widest number of businesses.

Newly designed inner city loan funds, newly designed inner city entrepreneurship centers: beyond these mechanisms, the policies to spur new inner city businesses are the same as those that are needed to spur other new businesses: keep government business taxes and business regulation to a minimum.

Five years ago I wouldn't have written these lines. But participation in running the six Renaissance businesses taught me how serious a drag on new business growth the taxes and regulation can be.

Among business taxes, the Social Security (Federal Insurance Contributions Act) payroll tax, currently at 7.15 percent of earnings paid by employers (with a matching share by employees) is the major impediment to job generation and business growth. In all of the Renaissance businesses, we sought to maximize job creation while keeping the business above break-even point. Repeatedly we found that the taxes, if small for one worker, amounted to nearly $1,000 per month for the ten workers in, say, the messenger service. This amount eroded the slim profit margin that the business existed on and discouraged additional hires.

More basically, given the nature of Social Security, there is no good reason why small janitorial companies or small messenger services, rather than the general tax base, should bear the cost. Social Security is not an annuity program. As the *New Republic* has noted, the money that today's retirees pay into the Social Security system over their lifetimes, invested at a normal rate of return, would pay for less than one-sixth of the benefits a typical retiree enjoys. Social Security is a transfer program; and it should find its support, like other transfer programs, from general revenues.

Government regulation also should be structured with greater awareness of the struggles of new businesses. The Renaissance convenience store ran up against regulation on a number of occasions. The local health inspector closed the store down for two days for selling coffee without the proper permit. Most disturbing was the attitude of the inspector: that we were committing a serious wrong in not possessing the permit, and that we should be shut down until it was obtained. What kind of a regulatory structure is this, that we should be on the defensive? The inspector has got a steady job and steady salary, while we're the ones struggling to meet payroll and create jobs.

Keeping taxes and regulation to a minimum are policies not usually on the agenda of the individuals and agencies concerned about inner city unemployment. They are not glamorous policies, and they are not the stuff of calls to the barricades. But they will result in jobs and in greater fairness to the risk-taking entrepreneurs.

"This inner city entrepreneurism is all a fad; it offers no serious solution to inner city unemployment," declares Professor Sar Levitan of George Washington University, one of the deans of job training policy in the United States. His view reflects that of many other leaders of the nation's liberal establishment in employment policy.

They represent the welfare state side of modern liberalism, and they are wrong. Perhaps only 15 percent of the total unemployed at any time are cut out to be entrepreneurs. But if that 15 percent launched enterprises, they would create hundreds of thousands of new enterprises across the nation.

For the great majority of the inner city unemployed—the welfare recipients, inner city young people, ex-offenders—their best chance lies in getting a steady job and building an economic base. However, even among the inner city unemployed, perhaps 10 percent are potential entrepreneurs. They possess the strong desire to operate a business, as well as the intuitive business sense to have a realistic chance of success. They are more fitted temperamentally to carve out their own jobs (and perhaps jobs for others) than to be one of twenty persons competing for a file clerk job in a downtown insurance agency. Why shouldn't they be encouraged to be more than an additional clerk applicant?

More numerous are the potential entrepreneurs among the general unemployed population and the persons in middle-or low-level jobs. Joyce Burris probably would be regarded by Professor Levitan as fortunate to have a legal secretary position that pays over $25,000. But she is willing to take a risk in starting a business (she wants to be more than an employee), and she has succeeded at least in winning a few contracts for her word processing.

Joyce's business is out of her apartment, but other entrepreneurs, like Darrell Mark, a disco owner, are locating in inner city areas. Still others, like Eric Jones, the chauffeur-turned-limousine-owner are hiring from the inner city unemployed.

Moreover, a good number of these potential entrepreneurs, like Joyce Burris and Darrell Mark, are black. The development of a strong black entrepreneurial sector is only a matter of time. It is growing slowly today. It will grow more rapidly as its importance is recognized and as entrepreneur assistance programs assume a more realistic form.

Which brings us back to Bill Walker and R. C. Monceaux. After his Black Like Me gallery showing in early 1986, Walker has continued to keep in touch with Entrepreneurship Center staff. Recognizing he may not be competitive in the corporate market, Walker has switched to marketing to individuals and has achieved a small flow of orders. He and his partner, Andre Taylor, are unlikely to become the world- traveling corporate and fashion photographers they dream of being. But if they do persevere in business, they can do better than the bus driver job or unemployment that would be the result of the Professor Levitan approach. Even the Black Like Me gallery owner, R. C. Monceaux, might slowly build a real gallery if he can identify more accurately a market for his art and take new steps to reach this market.

In *The Spirit of Enterprise,* George Gilder soars in his rhetoric on the virtues of the entrepreneur: "Entrepreneurs are optimists, who see in every path of sand a potential garden, in every man a potential worker, in every problem a possible profit. Their self-interest succumbs to their deeper interest and engagement in the world beyond themselves, impelled by their curiosity, imagination and faith." According to Gilder, entrepreneurs are "the hands that lift up the economy," for "their decision whether to invest...and the quality of their ideas determine the pace and substance of growth." Gilder notes that the establishment economists look at the economy and see only the money supply or the level of government spending as influencing jobs and the employment level; they ignore the entrepreneurial economy.

When Gilder speaks of entrepreneurs, he (like nearly all of other recent writers on entrepreneurship) means the men and women who start multi-million dollar companies—National Semiconductor Corporation, Micron Technology, Apple Computers. But his insight is apt for inner city communities.

The establishment economists and social scientists, like Levitan, look at inner city communities and see only social pathologies and large-scale government training or public service employment. They miss the entrepreneurial economy that is transforming the Mission district and other inner city areas. It is an economy that holds such promise, if only we can give rein to its power.

NOTES — The Possibilities for Inner City Entrepreneurship

1. David Birch, "Who Creates Jobs?," *Public Interest*, Fall 1981; David Birch, "The Job Generation Process: Final Report to the Economic Development Administration," Cambridge, Mass. MIT Program on Neighborhood Change, 1979.

2. Other leading research efforts that confirm the importance of new and small businesses in job generation are Catherine Armington and Marjorie Odle, "Sources of Recent Employment Growth: 1978-1980," Washington D.C., The Brookings Institute, 1982; Candee Harris, "Small Business and Job Generation: A Changing Economy or Differing Methodologies," Washington D.C., The Brookings Institute, 1983; and on the role of small businesses in California, Michael Teitz, "Small Business and Employment Growth in California," Berkeley, California, University of California, Department of City and Regional Planning, 1980.

3. Cognetics, "Analysis of Economic Growth and Change: San Francisco County: 1972-1984," Cambridge, Mass., Cognetics Inc., 1985.

4. Cognetics, "Denver/Boulder: Summary of Growth Trends 1972-1982," Cambridge, Mass., Cognetics Inc., 1985.

5. Joel Kotkin, "The Reluctant Entrepreneurs," *Inc.*, September 1986.

6. Beginning in 1965, the War on Poverty brought an emphasis on developing new minority-owned businesses and new businesses located in inner city areas. These businesses would expand business ownership. They also would generate much-needed jobs.

How could these businesses develop? New financing sources were needed argued a number of policy analysts. These analysts portrayed minority and inner city communities as suffering from a capital gap in the financing of new ventures. If financing were available, many would-be entrepreneurs could get started and succeed.

For example, W.J. Garvin, "The Small Business Capital Gap: The Special Case of Minority Enterprise," *Journal of Finance* May 1971, p.445-457; "Commercial Banks and Minority Entrepreneurship," *Yale Law Journal* 1971, p.614-646, Theodore Cross, *Black Capitalism*, New York, Atheneum, 1969.

The literature of the period also includes argument for the need to guide minority business development into new areas, for example, Samuel Doctors and Sharon Lockwood, "New Directions for Minority Enterprise," 36 *Law and Contemporary Problems*, 1971, ("high growth industries"); Anthony Pascal, "Black Gold and Black Capitalism," *Public Interest*, Spring 1970, p.111-119 ("black control of the service station industry").

7. Richard Klein, "Financial Results of the Small Business Administration's Minority Business Portfolio," *University of Michigan Business Review,* 1979, p.17-26.

8. Robert Edelstein, "Improving the Selection of Credit Risks: An Analysis of a Commercial Bank Minority Lending Program", *Journal of Finance,* March 1975, p.37-54.

9. One of the private loan funds was the Fund for United Negro Development in Boston. A description of the Fund is given by J. Anthony Lukas in his excellent account of urban turmoil in Boston during the 1970s, *Common Ground,* New York, Knopf, 1985. One of the main characters in the book, Ms. Rachel Twymons, a black woman on public assistance through much of the 1960s, was involved in a minority business development program. In 1966, Ms. Twymons was working as a part-time saleswoman at a clothing store near Dudley Square. The store owner decided to sell, and encouraged by the Small Business Administration, Ms. Twymons decided to buy. She received an SBA loan of $18,000.

Her store, "Rachel's Specialty Shop" opened in November 1967. It lasted through March 1969, when the initial capitalization had been spent. Fixtures and stock were sold at auction for $4,000 which went back to the SBA. Ms. Twymons abandoned a business career at this point.

Chapter 15

A Middlemarch Surgeon

For the past six years I have lived on Golden Gate Avenue in the city's Tenderloin district. The Tenderloin exemplifies the the varied population in our inner cities today, as well as the confusion of policy responses on both the left and the right.

Located in the middle of the city, between the financial district and Civic Center, the Tenderloin is the city's densest area, housing 20,000 persons. Like many inner city areas, its deterioration came after World War II, when its tourist hotels were turned into cheap residential hotels and urban renewal and displacement in other neighborhoods swelled its population. A 1980 survey found a median monthly household income of $559 for the apartment dwellers in the area and $433 for the residential hotel dwellers; 50 percent of the apartment dwellers and 75 percent of the hotel dwellers received state or federal income assistance.

Though the Tenderloin's population usually is described as the "inner city poor," it is really three populations: the elderly, the Indochinese refugees, and the down-and-outers. The elderly are mainly single males, retired longshoremen and merchant marines, living on pensions in the one-room studios that dominate the area. Few are looking for jobs, and except for hopes of winning the state lottery, few expect to move up economically.

In contrast, the Indochinese refugee population is moving up economically and out of the Tenderloin. The Southeast Asian population grew by over 800% between the 1970 and 1980 censuses. The refugee families are crowded seven or eight persons to a two-room apartment, but nobody doubts that these families soon will live in homes out in the Richmond or Sunset districts. Early in the mornings their children are on the bus corners, waiting for the school buses. Their local community agency, the Center for Southeast Asian Refugee Resettlement, is the envy of other community agencies for its new building. The center recently launched a loan fund to help finance new refugee businesses, and these businesses—restaurants, grocery stores, jewelry stores—are beginning to dot the area.

The third population, the down-and-outers, are the men (and a few women) who can be seen lining the street corners at all hours of the day and night. They eat at St. Anthony's Church, Glide Church, and the other soup kitchens in the area and sleep in the cheap residential hotels or the shelters. They live off SSI payments or welfare payments or the netherworld of prostitution and drugs.

They wear defeated or confused looks and are not competitive for the jobs opening up in the nearby downtown. Cutbacks in government housing or welfare subsidies are likely to lead them to further reliance on private charity, rather than spurring them to jobs and independence.

The local politicians talk about how terrible is this unemployment, and they blame Ronald Reagan. But few have any idea of what to do. The social service agencies scramble to do "needs assessments" and to criticize the local politicians (and Ronald Reagan) for "lacking compassion."

One exception is Leroy Looper, who operates the community organization, Reality House West. Reality House avoids the theoretical redistributionist debates. Instead, Looper concentrates on ways of building new wealth in the Tenderloin. He started by purchasing in 1977 the Cadillac Hotel, located in the heart of the Tenderloin on Eddy and Leavenworth. The Cadillac then was a dilapidated residential hotel, less than 20 percent occupied. He has turned it into a fully occupied venture, housing seniors, ex-offenders, and former patients of mental institutions. Last year he added a Sizzler restaurant on the ground floor. The Sizzler still is struggling financially, but it employs 40 to 50 persons as a job training venture.

All of this was done with a combination of government and private foundation funding. Without the government participation, the hotel and Sizzler would have been difficult to put together, if not impossible. But Leroy is not content to rely on government grants. Nor does he wait for large-scale government solutions, or think in terms of large-scale government bureaucracies. He is a builder, a developer of new wealth, a community entrepreneur. Like any good businessperson, he finds every opportunity to push his product. Whenever I see him, he is pushing the Sizzler ("Say, if you're having a meeting, why not do it at the Sizzler").

Throughout the city there are other community entrepreneurs, such as Leandro Soto, head of the job training agency Arriba Juntos. Soto has added a housing development and weatherization business to the job training. Soto and the other community entrepreneurs are working quietly, without the glamour of local politicians. But they are doing far more than the politicians in creating jobs and in building wealth.

Across the Bay, the inner city area of East Oakland often is pictured by sociologists as a "sick" community characterized by drugs and unemployment. But a closer look reveals considerable vitality and the community entrepreneurism that forms the basis for revitalization.

In early 1986 the Koshland Fund asked Sandy Close, the president of Pacific News Service, to visit East Oakland and recommend if private foundations should invest in the area. Close's report, "East Oakland: Pathways to Community Revitalization" recommended a foundation role that contrasted with the usual anti-poverty suggestions of training, organizing, or government job creation.

Close traced the loss of East Oakland's manufacturing base over the past 30 years. In the 1950s, East Oakland boasted a General Motors assembly plant, and a variety of canneries, and foundry works. By 1985 nearly all of these ventures had closed. The main business artery, East 14th Street, had become a series of vacant lots, wig shops, laundry houses, storefront churches, and liquor stores.

During the same time of 1950-1985, public housing units were built in East Oakland, and a low income, largely black population moved in. In 1985, Castlemont High, one of the area's main high schools, had a student body 94% black, and 91% from families receiving AFDC.

Despite the economic decline and welfare dependency, Close found most reason for hope in the actions of East Oakland community entrepreneurs, who were initiating projects on their own to build new wealth in the area. Eulah Brimson is a single parent who started an informal home day care center to make money. From this activity, she launched an association of local day care providers, leading to lower liability rates for each member. Marie Turner works as a housecleaner and janitor. She also has created a meal preparation project that feeds hundreds of seniors and creates work for other seniors. Al Parham is a former War on Poverty official, currently a small businessperson in East Oakland. He has created an association of the black businesspersons in East Oakland to target the jobs created at East Oakland youth.

None of these efforts has more than a tiny impact in jobs or businesses. They are pathetically small, and even if multiplied ten times would not begin to dent the unemployment and welfare dependency. But, Close argues, they indicate the individual initiative and wealth generation that is possible, and around which foundations and government should bring to bear their considerable resources.

These East Oakland efforts do point the way for a better anti-poverty policy. They and their values, and not the Great Society programs of the 1960s or the Reaganite programs of the 1980s, should be the future.

Restructured job training, new incentives for inner city work, welfare reform, and inner city entrepreneurism: these are the policies that will turn around our inner cities. And each is based on the same values, the values represented by Leroy Looper and the East Oakland community entrepreneurs: the values of the wealth builder, the job generator, the risk-taker.

These policies require government participation. None can be carried out to any significant degree with private funding or private charity. Yet, with these policies, government participation takes a different form than in the past. In East Oakland or the Tenderloin of San Francisco, the government's role would not be "How can we help these people; what can we give them." Rather it would be, "how can the unemployed and low income people help themselves carve out jobs and ownership".

The Leroy Loopers and East Oakland community entrepreneurs would be models, and government resources brought to bear to multiply their number many fold. As importantly, in thinking about job training or job creation in East Oakland or the Tenderloin, the first question would be "How can risk taking, market discipline, and wealth creation be built into the government program."

Stated another way, government funding would play an important role in reducing inner city dependency. To deny this, and rely on the free market alone would be wishful thinking. But government participation would take a different form than in the past. It would no longer mean the paternalism and bureaucracy of the Great Society programs. Rather, the new government participation would alter incentive structures in inner city communities, and help residents carve out ways of generating new wealth, not only redistributing wealth.

Traditional liberals are uncomfortable with talk of wealth creation or risk-taking or market discipline. "It's all a fad, this talk of entrepreneurism or risk-taking", says our friend Professor Sar Levitan, who helped design the Great Society programs of the 1960s and 1970s. But it's time that Levitan and his fellow liberals came down from their universities, and think tanks and government offices and served as job developers and inner city teachers and businesspersons on the local level.

They would find that their job training schemes, so fine in theory, have serious structural shortcomings. To a greater extent, they would see that these schemes and other liberal government schemes do not adequately address the work disincentives and discouragements in low income communities.

If Levitan and other liberals ever worked on the local level, they quickly would turn away from the Great Society mindset, and recognize how government's role must change.

They also would recognize that changes must come in the way that government policy is constructed. A willingness to start small and build on successes, and a willingness to learn from community-based work should be the touchstones of policy formulation.

During the 1960s War on Poverty, millions of dollars flowed to community groups that had not been strengthened and hardened with experience. These groups were not required to start small, and build on successes, as private businesses are required to do.

Further, persons who seek to lead on the national or state levels should be expected to spend at least four to five years on local programs. The Joe Califano or Stuart Eizenstat who believes he can move from a Washington law firm to a policymaking position should be rejected.

Today, prominent liberal Democrats like Califano and Eizenstat, who designed inner city strategy in the Carter Administration, are models for many bright young men and women, seeking a policymaking career. What a great distortion of reality, I discovered. These men, with their olympian careers, lack true experience and can contribute little to effective policy.

When I returned from Washington, D.C. in early 1985, I was more than ever convinced of the value of local experience, and I tried to convey this value to my students at U.C. Berkeley. I tried to emphasize how daily work in a local job training agency, though seemingly mundane, did have major policy value. The role of the job developer, for example, involves calling and meeting with employers for job openings, and keeping in contact with employers and training graduates to ensure successful job placements. In the short run, these efforts seem to teach nothing. Yet, over a period of time working as a job developer, one comes to understand the obstacles to reducing inner city unemployment far better than one can by reading a sociology tract or a Bureau of Labor Statistics report.

My arguments for local experience stirred little interest among the students until the day I showed them an article by Stuart Eizenstat. A number of the graduate students had heard of Eizenstat and knew that he was President Carter's main domestic advisor. Eizenstat's article focused on the need for new inner city employment initiatives. He recited the familiar statistics of inner city unemployment, welfare dependency, and female headed households. He then announced that steps must be taken promptly to resolve the problems of welfare mothers and of the "young poor male".

However, the policy recommendations that followed were no more than a vague call for action: "community intervention programs," "youth employment demonstration programs", a "guaranteed job program for young people in high dropout areas," and my favorite, a"federal, state, and private sector partnership to provide opportunity for these young men and truly solve their problem." To show that he wasn't one more sentimental liberal, Eizenstat had added the requirement that "welfare benefits should be tied directly to work and job training." without saying how this was to be accomplished.

Would the students recognize how empty Eizenstat's suggestions were? Many did. We discussed how a college undergraduate could put together a policy laundry list similar to Eizenstat's, and how poorly Eizenstat's fine resume had served him in policy development. In the next weeks, I was pleased to find students frequently asking about local anti- poverty opportunities.

One night about the same time, my wife Donna and I met Dick Neustadt for a drink at the Carnelian Room in downtown San Francisco. I had admired Neustadt's work in policy analysis since I first met him at Harvard in the early 1970s. During the spring semester, he was a visiting professor at U.C. Berkeley.

In discussing employment policy, he told me that I was too hard on Califano and Eizenstat. He knew them both, and considered them good, serious men who brought a great deal of intelligence to the policy process. Sitting in the Carnelian Room, located on the fifty-second floor of the Bank of America building, I stared at the lights of San Francisco spreading from the Golden Gate Bridge to the East Bay and thought, what the hell, why worry about Joe Califano and his influence. But later, away from the Carnelian Room glamour and back in the low income Mission district, I knew that there was good reason to take seriously Califano's poor example.

Attracting aspiring policymakers to the local level will not be easy. All of the incentives of money, prestige, and job advancement are weighted toward working at the national level. Prized jobs include being the "Special Assistant to the Special Assistant of the Secretary of Health and Human Resources", or the "Deputy Counsel of the Senate Labor Committee". These jobs do not include working in a community-based organization, in the same low income neighborhood every day.

One can imagine a different system in which aspiring policymakers are expected, if not required, to work on the local

level before coming to Washington. They would spend four to
five years in local employment, health or housing organizations,
and come to understand the subtleties of issues and the
problems of implementation. In the employment field they
would learn, for example, how job training funds really are distributed and administered, how local labor markets operate,
and what incentives encourage the hiring of the inner city unemployed. They would go beyond the "paper scenery" to understand the realities of finding work for the unemployed.

In the Mission district, it is sometimes difficult to see beyond
the daily issues of job placements and the life crises among job
seekers. But across the city, on the edge of the Bay, the use of
imagination is easier.

At the base of the Golden Gate Bridge, there is a little-traveled
path that winds upward to the Bridge towers. Ascending, the
city spreads out before you. At the top is a plaque placed at the
dedication of the Bridge in 1937.

Throughout the nineteenth century, the construction of a
bridge linking San Francisco and Marin was thought technical-
ly impossible, if not far too expensive. But an American engineer,
Joseph Strauss, not only designed a bridge but persevered for a
decade to convince the local officials. What he built not only was
a bridge of great beauty and utility, but also a monument to
faith. Its immense Art Deco towers testify to the quality of belief,
the ability to think big and imagine a future. The plaque dedi-
cates the Bridge to the "adventurous spirit" and proclaims,

> Lifting its mighty form high above the Golden Gate
> the Bridge shall testify to the faith and devotion of those
> who, undaunted through the years
> Sought honestly and fairly through this structure
> To tender a definite contribution

To the cultural heritage of mankind.

Looking across the Bridge, I can imagine a future of employment far removed from today's inner city unemployment and dependency. It is a future in which far more people enjoy a productive place in the workforce. Government does not become a major employer, rather government stimulates a healthy and expanding private sector. Business ownership is more widespread, and potential entrepreneurs from all classes and races are actively sought out, encouraged, and urged to persevere if they meet initial failures. Anthony Johnson and Louise Allen are not "superfluous workers": they have jobs to go to every day, they possess skills valued in the work, and perhaps someday they become owners and employers.

There is a job, a place in the workforce, even for Patrick Martin. Although he has not been to Renaissance in three years, hardly a month goes by that I don't think of him. He was not one of Renaissance's success stories: we were unable to place him in a job outside of Renaissance, and laid him off after a short time at our Renaissance Cleaners. His life and unemployment, though, bore a heartbreaking quality not easily forgotten.

His job goals were modest. He wanted janitorial work ("scrubbing floors, sweeping, you know, I can do that"). At the Renaissance Cleaners, he missed two work assignments. The Cleaners' general manager, under pressure to make the business succeed (and not lose customers), did not have time to try bringing along Patrick.

After Patrick was laid off by the Cleaners, I sought to find him another job. An appointment was arranged with the personnel director at American Building Maintenance, the large janitorial firm. The personnel director called shortly thereafter to report that Patrick appeared on time, but could not pass the basic reading test. "Even for janitorial work," the personnel director explained, "you have to know how to read and write to mix solutions. Patrick could hurt himself or others if he can't read the instructions." What of enrolling in a literacy class? Patrick did not want to return to a classroom, he wanted a job.

As Renaissance grew, gradually I saw him less and less. When I called after a few months, his mother's phone was disconnected, with no forwarding number.

Though Patrick usually was easy-going, one of the last times I saw him, he expressed unhappiness about his situation. He didn't like the noise in the household, and people coming and in and out at all hours. He didn't like the money-making deals they talked about ("they have bad thoughts"). He didn't like that other young men in the neighborhood made fun of him. He talked of getting a janitorial job and moving out to a new neighborhood in San Francisco or in the East Bay, where he could meet new people ("You know, people who are nice").

A hundred years ago, a Golden Gate bridge was thought too visionary. Is it any more visionary to imagine an organization of work in which Patrick can find janitorial work, and move to a nicer neighborhood?

The day after Christmas 1985 a large crate was delivered to Renaissance. It contained a polished brass train bell, mounted on a wood base. It was a present to Renaissance from David Smith.

Smith was the president of Chemical Exchange Company in Houston, a multi-million dollar chemical refining company. He was conservative Republican who regarded unemployment as the source of most social ills. "A man who doesn't have a job naturally feels bad about himself. We all need to feel productive." Working through his church, and with his own money, he had started a small restaurant at the local YMCA and a job placement service for men on the local skid row. He rejected the idea of unemployment at 6% or 7% and spoke of unemployment at 2% or 3%.

In other cities across the United States I have met men and women like David Smith who are not resigned to unemployment at 6% or above, and who want to do more than call for more jobs. So much can be done if their business skills and the varied skills of others can be applied to training and job creation.

We will not reach all of the unemployed. Some always will be seeking shortcuts, not interested in working up the job ladders. Others will have emotional problems and not fit into the organization of work. They will be the minority. More can be integrated into steady jobs.

"But he did not simply aim at a more genuine kind of practice than was common," wrote George Eliot of the doctor Lydgate who worked in the provinces but sought to contribute to science. "He was ambitious of a wider effect, he was fired with the possibility that he might work out the proof of an anatomical conception and make a link in the chain of discovery." And Eliot added, "Does it seem incongruous to you that a Middlemarch surgeon should dream of himself as a discoverer."

Let us be Middlemarch surgeons, day to day working on the local level, on specific projects. Let us also be discoverers, striving to better give reign to the talents of all Americans for a stronger economy and a stronger America.

Bibliography

In understanding today's inner city unemployment and poverty, the following accounts of this unemployment and of various attempts to reduce it are valuable starting points:

Auletta, Ken *The Underclass*, New York, Random House, 1982.

Bane, Mary Jo and David Ellwood, "The Dynamics of Dependence", Cambridge, Mass., Urban Systems Research, 1983.

Berlin, Gordon, *Not Working: Unskilled Youth and Displaced Adults*, New York, Ford Foundation, 1983.

Brown, Claude, "Manchild in Harlem", *New York Times Magazine,* September 26, 1984.

Burtless, Gary, "Manpower Policies for the Disadvantaged: What Works", *Brookings Review,* Fall 1984.

Freeman, Richard, "Young Blacks and Jobs: What We Know Now", *Public Interest,* Winter 1985.

Gilder, George, *Visible Man,* New York, Basic Books, 1978.

Gueron, Judith, "Reforming Welfare With Work", New York, Manpower Demonstration Research Corporation, 1987.

Hahn, Andrew and Robert Lerman, *What Works in Youth Employment Policy*, Washington D.C., Committee on New American Realities, 1985.

Kaus, Mickey, "The Work Ethic State", *The New Republic,* July 7, 1986.

Lefkowitz, Bernard, *Tough Change,* New York, Free Press, 1987.

Lerman, Robert, "Who Are the Young Absent Fathers?", *Youth and Society,* September 1986.

Levy, Frank, "How Big is the American Underclass?", Washington D.C., Urban Institute, 1977.

Liebow, Elliot, *Tally's Corner,* Boston, Little, Brown, 1967.

Lukas, J. Anthony, *Common Ground,* New York, Knopf, 1985.

Mead, Lawrence, *Beyond Entitlement,* New York, Free Press, 1986.

Mead, Lawrence, "The Potential for Work Enforcement: A Study of WIN", New York, New York University, 1987.

Moynihan, Daniel Patrick, *Family and Nation,* New York, Harcourt Brace Jovanovich, 1986.

Murray, Charles, "White Welfare Families", *National Review,* March 28, 1986.

Nathan, Richard, "The Underclass—Will It Always Be With Us?", Princeton University, 1986.

Wilson, William Julius Kathyrn Neckerman, "Poverty and Family Structure" in Sheldon Danziger, *Fighting Poverty: What Works and What Doesn't,* Cambridge, Harvard University Press, 1986.

Roger Wilkins, *A Man's Life,* New York, Simon & Schuster, 1982.

Index

About the Author

In 1982 Michael Bernick, an attorney, left a position in a downtown San Francisco law firm to head the San Francisco Renaissance Center, a new inner city job training and business development center. *Urban Illusions* is a personal account of the Center's attempts to increase inner city employment over the next five years.

Urban Illusions is the second of a multi-volume series planned by Mr. Bernick on employment and unemployment in America. The first volume, *The Dreams of Jobs,* was published in 1984 and followed participants of job training programs from the 1960s and 1970s to the present.

Mr. Bernick did his undergraduate work at Harvard, and graduate work at Oxford University (Balliol College) and the University of California at Berkeley. Since 1984, he has been a member of the faculty at the University of California at Berkeley, Graduate School of Public Policy.